A WOMAN'S GUIDE TO INVESTING

VIRGINIA B. MORRIS AND **KENNETH M. MORRIS**
Authors of the best-selling
Wall Street Journal Guide to Understanding Money & Investing

with an introduction by
BRIDGET A. MACASKILL
CEO OppenheimerFunds

Developed in collaboration with
the *Women & Investing* experts
at OppenheimerFunds, Inc.

LIGHTBULB
PRESS

LIGHTBULB PRESS:
Corporate Staff
Chief Operating Officer Dean Scharf
Sales and Marketing Carol E. Davis, Germaine Ma, Karen Meldrom

Project Team
Design Director Dave Wilder
Production Janice Edelman, Chris Hiebert, Sally Minker, Thomas Trojan, Kwee Wang
Illustration Krista K. Glasser
Digital Output Quad Right, Inc.

SPECIAL THANKS TO:
Rob Densen, Elizabeth Brickman, Patricia Foster, Jane Ingalls, Mitchell Lindauer, Cathleen Meere Stahl

PICTURE CREDITS:
Alan Rosenberg, New York (pages 62, 63)

Women will come to this book with a wide range of experiences. They may be single or married, career women or full-time moms, 18 or 80. But one thing all women share is the need to secure their own financial futures.

Prepared or not, nine out of ten women will be responsible for their own finances at some point in their lives. Make no mistake about it, your financial future is up to you. Not your employer. Not your husband. Not the government.

The good news is that whatever your circumstances, there's plenty you can do right now to plan for your financial future. And, contrary to popular belief, you don't need a lot of money to be an investor. Whether you tackle your finances alone or with the help of a financial advisor, the trick is to get started now. This book can help.

Since conducting our groundbreaking 1992 research on women's attitudes about money and investing, we've talked to thousands of women across the country about their financial circumstances and concerns. This book is the result of those conversations. Initially released in 1997, the text has been revised and updated and includes recent tax law and other changes.

It is a book written with you in mind. A book that anticipates women's specific concerns, interests and life circumstances. A book that breaks through the confusing financial jargon. A book that understands the competing demands on your time. A book, we hope, that will empower you to take command of your financial future.

From wherever you are to wherever you want to go in life, this book will give you the understanding, confidence and encouragement you need to get there.

Bridget A. Macaskill
CEO OppenheimerFunds

A WOMAN'S GUIDE TO INVESTING

Financial Security

Achieving financial security is one of the most important challenges facing women today.

Financial security. It's something that most women spend a lot of time worrying about. "Will I have enough money?" "What should I do with the money I have?" "Should I be making investment decisions?"

Unfortunately, when it comes to actually investing, many women procrastinate. Perhaps overwhelmed by the alternatives, they do the simple thing: nothing. Sound familiar? If so, you're not alone. But there's something you can do. By learning as much as you can and getting sound financial advice, you'll be ready to build your future.

YOU CAN PAY THE RENT
If you're looking for help, you can find it. Investment seminars tailored for women are offered around the country, and financial advisors are increasingly attuned to working with women clients.

TAKING RESPONSIBILITY

While women in past generations could often avoid making financial decisions, women today can't. What's changed? For one thing, women are marrying later or not at all. And Americans, women in particular, are living longer.

So there's a good chance you'll spend 20 years or more in retirement. At the same time, responsibility for providing retirement income has shifted from the government and employers to the individual. Your mother or grandmother perhaps can rely on Social Security and her husband's pension to support her during retirement. You probably can't.

The best way to ensure that you'll have the money you'll need later is to start putting your finances in order today. Take it slowly. Learn a little bit at a time and don't worry too much. But start.

A WINNING RECORD

The good news is that women have what it takes to be smart investors. Many are actively involved, getting professional advice, buying mutual funds and investing for retirement in record numbers. And they're building the confidence they need to invest more assertively.

When you're ready to join their ranks—and the sooner the better, experts agree—you'll find that defining your goals and choosing the investments to meet them is challenging but not intimidating—and certainly within your grasp.

INVESTMENTS: THE KEY TO SECURITY

An investment is something you buy because you expect to make money on it, either because it increases in value or produces income, or both. You can put your money into **securities**, a term that refers to investments like stocks, bonds, and mutual funds. Or you might invest in a home, other real estate, or a number of other things that increase in value.

INVESTMENT SAVVY

As a woman, you don't need different investment advice than a man does. But you do need to consider the financial responsibilities you're likely to face and make plans to cope with them. The fact is, nine out of ten women will be solely responsible for managing their finances at some point in their adult lives. They need to be ready to do it.

Whether you are 25 or 75, a housewife or a career woman, now is the time to start learning about investing and building a portfolio that will provide the financial security you need for yourself and your loved ones.

The Gender Issue

Gender equality is the law in some things, but it can be an elusive goal where financial security is concerned.

A woman's need for financial security is no different from a man's. Achieving it is another story. Women tend to earn less than men and live longer. And they tend to invest more cautiously, which usually means less profitably.

Fortunately, the future is looking brighter. Women increasingly recognize that investing plays a decisive role in meeting financial goals. They're growing more confident about making smart investment decisions. And they're getting the help they need from professional advisors.

Earning Power

THE FACTS

Women often earn less than men because they work in lower-paying jobs or only part time. What's more, women tend to be paid 60% to 80% of what men earn for doing the same job, even when they have the same qualifications. Women also change jobs more frequently, which means they accumulate less retirement credit. And approximately 20% of adult women don't earn a paycheck, and may not have the financial security to survive divorce or widowhood.

THE SOLUTIONS

When it comes to investing, a woman's earning power is equal to a man's. That's why it is so important for women to invest. It's one way to close the existing gap between the earning potential of men and women.

While women have achieved some gains in salary parity in recent years, that alone will not provide them with long-term financial security. But if they put as much as they can into employer-sponsored retirement plans, start investing on their own and don't tap into those funds when they change jobs, that *will* make a difference.

WOMEN	Average salaries	MEN
$23,719		$32,144

Source: U.S. Bureau of the Census, 1996

Investing Styles

THE FACTS

Women as a group tend to be more conservative than men in choosing investments, and less willing to take the risks that they believe can come with investing. For example, single women save only 1.5% of their annual income and put less than 14.6% of their investment assets in **equities**, such as stocks, and in stock mutual funds, which historically are the most profitable. Women are also less apt to participate in voluntary retirement savings plans at work.

THE SOLUTIONS

Women who save regularly, learn as much as they can about investing, and create a financial plan for putting money into equities in a systematic, goal-oriented way can build their financial security.

Most people—women included—benefit from working with a financial advisor, both in drawing up an overall plan and identifying specific investments. One advantage of getting expert help is that it can be a great motivator, encouraging even the most reluctant to invest.

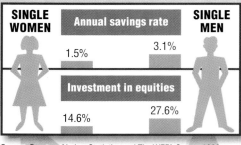

SINGLE WOMEN	Annual savings rate	SINGLE MEN
1.5%		3.1%
	Investment in equities	
14.6%		27.6%

Source: Bureau of Labor Statistics and The WEFA Group, 1993

Gender Roles

THE FACTS

Family dynamics have frequently put the man in the role of chief breadwinner and financial decision maker. As a result, women often doubt their own financial abilities or are reluctant to make investment decisions because they feel they lack experience or don't know enough.

Even women who manage the family checkbook are frequently not involved in investment or other long-term financial decisions. That's even more true when women don't have income of their own and are dependent on a husband or partner.

THE SOLUTIONS

In recent years, many women have taken a more active role in family financial affairs, especially as they've contributed more of the income. Women who have satisfying jobs are more likely to make joint financial decisions with their husbands. So are those who seek help from financial advisors, either independently or with their husbands. Obviously, the more knowledgeable women are about money, the less intimidated they'll be about participating.

Traditional resistance seems to be disappearing, too. The overwhelming majority of men in a survey for OppenheimerFunds—85%—agree that investing isn't solely a man's job.

WOMEN	Handle investment decisions	MEN
15%	38%	

	Handle day-to-day finances	
58%	42%	

Source: OppenheimerFunds, 1997

Life Expectancy

THE FACTS

Because women have historically earned less and lived longer, it's not surprising that a disproportionate 75% of the elderly poor are women. At age 65, women outnumber men three to two, and at 85 they outnumber them five to two, according to Census Bureau figures for 1994.

At the same time, fewer women have pensions (especially women over age 40), and they will qualify for less income from Social Security. Women also have fewer investments in their own right. Given their traditional investing patterns, women who retire in the next 20 years may well have less than one third of what they will need to live comfortably.

THE SOLUTIONS

If women invest more, and emphasize investments that will grow in value, they can make big strides toward having enough income when they need it.

Retirement planning is different for men and women, too. Because women, on average, live longer, they need more long-term resources. That's something that women and financial professionals must be clearer about.

Married women should be involved in decisions about their husbands' pension payouts and other financial arrangements, since they are likely to be faced with managing and investing this money. The time to learn about these matters is when the decisions are being made, not years afterward.

For similar reasons, a divorced woman should know about the rights she has to pension benefits and Social Security income based on her former husband's earnings.

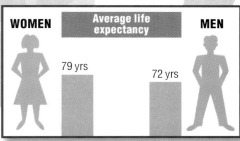

WOMEN	Average life expectancy	MEN
79 yrs	72 yrs	

Source: National Center for Health Statistics

Myth #1: Someone Will Watch Over Me

The biggest myth of all may be that women don't have to worry about money.

One of the comforting things about a myth is that it can cast a rosy glow around the realities of life. And for many people, the expectation that they'll live happily ever after once they're married has achieved mythic proportions.

The reality is that on average, a woman today spends more of her adult life unmarried than married—the consequence of later marriages, more divorces and widowhood. And she spends more years taking care of her parents than taking care of her children.

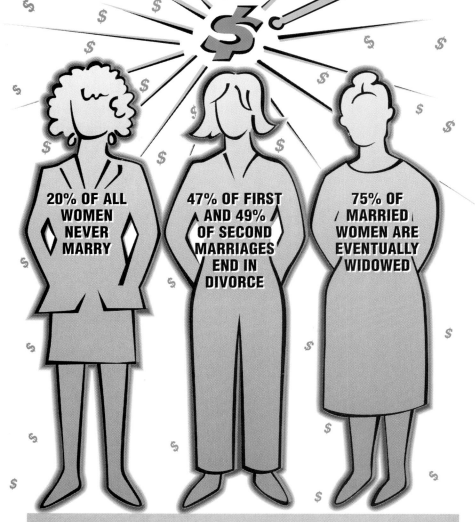

20% OF ALL WOMEN NEVER MARRY

47% OF FIRST AND 49% OF SECOND MARRIAGES END IN DIVORCE

75% OF MARRIED WOMEN ARE EVENTUALLY WIDOWED

HARD NUMBERS
There's an eye-opening difference between the financial security that a typical married couple family enjoys, compared with a woman-headed household or a single older woman.

Source: U.S. Bureau of the Census, 1996

Average family income:

Married couple	$49,858
Woman-headed household	$21,564
Older single women	$9,626

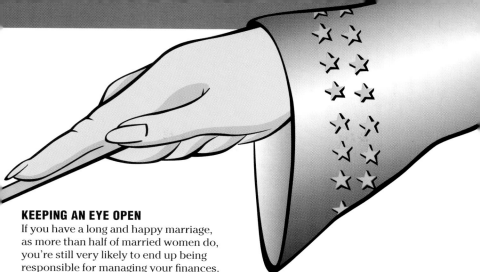

KEEPING AN EYE OPEN

If you have a long and happy marriage, as more than half of married women do, you're still very likely to end up being responsible for managing your finances. Nine out of every ten women are in that position at some point in their lives, many of them as older adults.

Throughout your marriage, it pays to be actively involved in any decisions your husband makes that will affect your financial security if he dies.

For example, will you continue to get income from his pension during your lifetime? The law requires some retirement plans to continue to pay benefits that he was entitled to for your lifetime or some specified period unless you agree to collect nothing so your husband gets larger payments while he's alive. Before you sign your share away, however, you should know what provision is being made for your future if you don't have a pension of your own (see page 146).

In a similar vein, if your husband plans to put his assets in trust for you, you need to know how much control you'll have over the income or principal. Decisions that save you the worry of managing money may tie your hands, and make your financial decisions dependent on a trustee's approval.

Without investment income you control, you may find it hard to afford to live as you wish.

THE REALITY OF DIVORCE

With divorce, women also have added responsibility for their long-term financial security. Those who don't have an investment plan in place will have to start from scratch—and learn the basics during a time of potential stress.

The financial impact of divorce hits women hard. On average, families headed by women have 44% of the income of married couples. That's true in part because there's been a gradual decrease in the number of women receiving property settlements, and a growing tendency to cap or end alimony payments.

Maintaining Financial Independence

Not everyone has a full-time job. But in most cases, taking responsibility for your financial security means having a regular source of income. Here are some ways to increase savings or boost your income:

 Can you work part-time to hold onto retirement plan opportunities?

 Can you learn a new skill or adapt the skills you have to the job market you'll go back into?

 Why not develop strategies with your husband to put certain assets in your name or invest in your own mutual fund or brokerage account?

 Or why not create a spousal IRA (see page 136)? Up to $2,000 a year can be salted away in your name even if you're not earning a salary—as a result of a new law that took effect in 1997.

 What about working from your home?

Myth #2: I Don't Have Enough Money to Invest

You've got it backwards. You don't have enough money *not* to invest.

The myth that you need a lot of money to start investing is just plain wrong. You can find a wide range of investment opportunities, and you can start small.

Mutual funds, for instance, often let you invest as little as $25 at a time if you agree to have the money automatically **debited**, or taken out of your savings or checking account. Banks and credit unions also offer a variety of incentives for investing through them.

Typical Expenses

Though everyone allocates income a little differently, depending on what they earn and what their priorities are, there are some recognizable patterns in what people spend for regular living expenses. According to recent government estimates, a typical budget might look something like this:

Expense categories	Typical expenses $25,000 income	$75,000 income
Housing	$10,500	$31,500
Food	$4,475	$13,425
Transportation	$4,275	$12,825
Health	$1,550	$4,650
Clothing	$1,255	$4,575
Entertainment	$1,100	$3,300
Other	$1,575	$4,725
Investment	**$0**	**$0**

Source: Bureau of Labor Statistics, 1992

FINDING INVESTMENT MONEY

When you realize how crucial it is to invest, you can almost always find the money to do it. One way is by trimming living expenses

SEVEN WAYS TO INVEST MORE

Here are several approaches to investing more of your income. They're fairly painless—and they work.

1 Don't buy the next thing you plan to put on your credit card. Go without it, and put that amount in your investment account.

2 Pay off the balance on your credit cards, and start putting an amount equal to the monthly interest payments in a special investment account.

3 Take advantage of any retirement contribution plan that's available at your job. Start putting money into it as soon as you can.

ONE STEP AT A TIME

You'll probably find the slow, steady approach works best for building your investments. You might start by putting money into a mutual fund on a regular basis (see page 80). And you can add not only your planned contributions, but any extra you have to invest. Your money can start growing immediately, and it's less apt to get spent than it would if it were fattening up your checking account.

Since investments in the average mutual fund have historically grown faster than savings accounts, and since you can easily sell shares in the fund if you need the money, a fund is often a smarter long-term investment.

5% HERE AND 5% THERE

You swear you can't afford 5% of your income for investment? Think about it this way: if you're earning $40,000, you're talking about $38.50 a week, or $5.50 a day. If you wrote your investment account a check for 5% of your weekly income each Monday morning you'd probably never miss it, and you'd have a lot to show for your effort.

YOUR CALL

It's a mistake to think you don't have enough to invest. The tighter your budget, the more you're going to need the extra income that investments provide. While being disciplined enough to build your account regularly can be tough, you can do it if you decide you're going to.

Reorganized Expenses

If your goal is to invest 10% of your income—an amount many financial experts urge you to aim for—you could reduce several expense categories by a small percent to produce the money. The numbers below suggest how that approach would affect a typical budget:

Expense categories	Typical expenses	
	$25,000 income	$75,000 income
Housing	$10,500	$31,500
Food	$3,975	$11,925
Transportation	$3,775	$11,325
Health	$1,550	$4,650
Clothing	$1,025	$3,075
Entertainment	$600	$1,800
Other	$1,075	$3,225
Investment	$2,500	$7,500

a little here and a little there. Of course, there are some things that are difficult to cut—like your mortgage or health insurance. But others are often more flexible. If you take a hard look at where your money is going, you might be surprised at how easy it is to find the areas where you can conserve.

Expense categories REDUCED to create investment amount

4 Invest automatically by having a percentage of your salary deducted from your paycheck—or write a check to your investment account every month when you pay your bills.

5 Invest some—or all—of any extra money you get from gifts, bonuses, or additional jobs.

6 Avoid having too much withheld for taxes. If you got a refund last year, see if you can reduce your withholding. Put the difference into your investment account or a retirement plan where you work.

7 Reinvest all the money you earn on the investments you have, preferably automatically, so you're not tempted to spend it.

Myth #3: I Don't Have Enough Time

Investing doesn't take as much time as you think—and it's time well spent.

You're probably too busy. And you have different responsibilities competing for your attention. But the truth is, you can always find time for the important things. Your financial security, and the security of your loved ones, is one of the most important.

Getting started with investing does take some time, since you have to define your goals and decide how to meet them. But once you've begun, you'll find it takes very little time to keep things rolling. And as your nest egg starts to grow, you'll realize the time you've put into investing is time well spent.

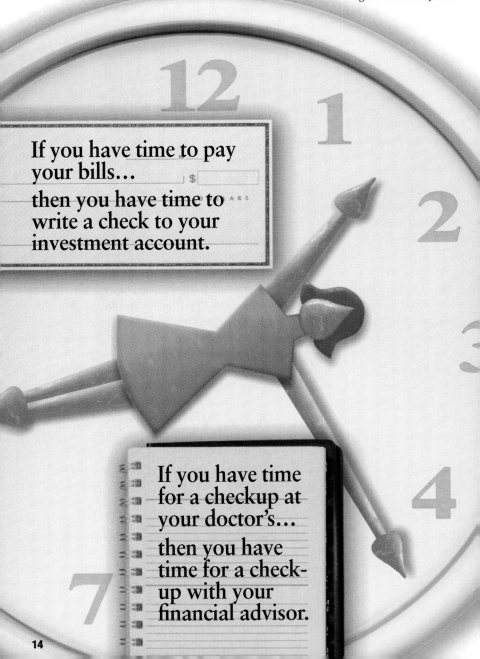

If you have time to pay your bills... then you have time to write a check to your investment account.

If you have time for a checkup at your doctor's... then you have time for a checkup with your financial advisor.

FITTING INVESTING IN

Think about all the things you do every month because they have to get done. Paying your bills is probably at the top of the list—unless you've arranged to have most of them paid directly from your bank account. Investing is actually a lot like paying bills. But instead of paying for past expenses, you're making a down payment on your financial future.

You can get serious about investing in several ways. For example, you can invest from every paycheck automatically, or you can contribute every month, or every opportunity you get. The appeal of automatic contributions is that you don't have to think about it. But investing on your own gives you the flexibility of putting in more when you can, or skipping an occasional payment if you must.

> If you have time to do the crossword puzzle...
> then you have time to read the financial column.

TIME IS MONEY

Regular additions to your investment accounts are the surest way to build financial security. Remember, once money is invested, it can continue to grow on its own. And the longer it's invested, the more your money can grow.

For example, by investing $2,000 a year for just ten years in your 20s, you can build a bigger nest egg than you can by investing $2,000 every year from age 30 to age 65.

And if you start early and stick with it, a $2,000 investment every year for 30 years—or $60,000— could provide you with $244,692 before taxes if you earned an average of 8% per year and reinvested all your earnings.*

The average American spends...

 4 hours a week cooking

 9 hours a week eating

 8 hours a week on household chores

 13 hours a week on child and pet care

 5 hours a week reading

 6 hours a week commuting

 18 hours a week watching television

2 hours a week exercising

52 hours a week sleeping

...but how many hours a week on personal finance?

Source: New York Times, 1995

Myth #4: I Don't Know Enough About Investing

You can't avoid a financial crisis by keeping your head in the sand.

To a beginner, investing can be a daunting task. Part of the reason is the lingo—just what is a tax-deferred salary reduction plan anyway?

Some women may have the impression that investors belong to a special club. If you have to ask how it works, you might be afraid you don't belong.

Or it may be that some women are afraid they don't know enough to make smart investment decisions.

If you want to learn, you've come to the right place. In the following chapters, you'll find the information you need to ask the right questions, understand the answers, and make some smart investment decisions.

BASIC TRAINING
There are some investment basics that every investor needs to know:

Stocks represent ownership shares in a corporation, and may pay dividends

Bonds pay interest over a specific period of time

Mutual funds pool your money with that of other investors to buy stocks, bonds or other investments

The reality of financial markets is that nobody can be sure how any investment will perform in the future. But while this uncertainty is never comfortable, remember that as an investor, history is on your side if you invest for the long term.

For example, over the past 70 years, equity investments on average have increased in value in most years. And during that time, there's been no 15- or 20-year period when stocks haven't made money, according to the research firm Ibbotson Associates.**

GROUP DYNAMICS
There are lots of great reasons to join—or create—an investment club. Several heads can be better than one, and pooled money buys more. Interestingly, in recent years, all-women's clubs and clubs with both men and women have out-numbered and outperformed all-male clubs, according to The National Association of Investors Corporation (NAIC) of Madison Heights, MI. You can contact them for informa-tion and guidelines. The phone number is 248-583-6242.

BUILDING YOUR EXPERTISE
Investing is a lot like exercise: you may have to talk yourself into starting. But once you've made your initial investment, you can build your expertise gradually.

If you're just starting, you might choose one or two mutual funds to build some equity. As you grow more confident,

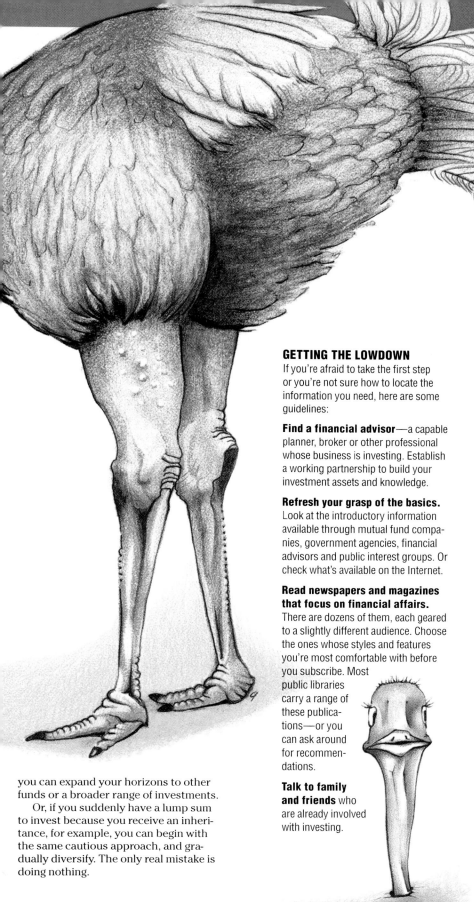

GETTING THE LOWDOWN

If you're afraid to take the first step or you're not sure how to locate the information you need, here are some guidelines:

Find a financial advisor—a capable planner, broker or other professional whose business is investing. Establish a working partnership to build your investment assets and knowledge.

Refresh your grasp of the basics. Look at the introductory information available through mutual fund companies, government agencies, financial advisors and public interest groups. Or check what's available on the Internet.

Read newspapers and magazines that focus on financial affairs. There are dozens of them, each geared to a slightly different audience. Choose the ones whose styles and features you're most comfortable with before you subscribe. Most public libraries carry a range of these publications—or you can ask around for recommendations.

Talk to family and friends who are already involved with investing.

you can expand your horizons to other funds or a broader range of investments.

Or, if you suddenly have a lump sum to invest because you receive an inheritance, for example, you can begin with the same cautious approach, and gradually diversify. The only real mistake is doing nothing.

Myth #5: A Good Advisor Is Hard to Find

Good investment advice is rarely more than a phone call away.

If you're like most people, you may be looking for someone who can lay out your choices and help you make important financial decisions.

There are good reasons for getting professional investment advice, just as there are good reasons for consulting a doctor when you need medical care. Financial advisors can explain how different kinds of investments have performed in the past, since that's an indication—though not a promise—of how they may do in the future. Advisors can also describe different approaches to investing, from conservative to aggressive, to help you gauge what's best for you.

On a more personal level, an advisor can help you define your financial goals and estimate how much money you'll need to meet them. Together, you can create a financial plan and choose investments in an effort to make it work. When you've pinpointed the kind of financial advice you need, you can find someone with particular expertise (see page 52).

ADVISORS YOU CAN CONSULT

- **Financial planners**
- **Stockbrokers**
- **Insurance agents**
- **Bank investment reps**
- **Certified Public Accountants**

A GENDER BOND?

Should you be looking for a woman advisor? A majority of women investors in an OppenheimerFunds survey say that gender isn't a factor when they decide which advisor to work with. Their primary concern is that it's someone who takes them seriously and treats them with respect.

PYRAMIDS AND OTHER SCAMS

How about an investment that promises to make you rich quick? If it involves a lot of money and little information, it's not an investment. It's a con-game.

Even though Charles Ponzi's infamous pyramid, promising a 40% return, collapsed decades ago, clever schemes surface all the time. Sadly, many of them are marketed to older people, especially women. There are plenty of tales of otherwise careful people who lose their shirts.

The best defense? Realistic expectations, healthy skepticism, and professional advice.

ELEMENTS OF A STRONG RELATIONSHIP

In the past, women have sometimes reported negative experiences with financial advisors they've consulted, such as feeling they were being ignored, talked down to, or not taken as seriously as men investors. But an OppenheimerFunds survey of women currently working with a financial advisor demonstrates that things have changed for the better.

Most important, **95%** of the women in the survey said that they are pleased with the advice they're getting, and **97%** said they trust their advisors. The findings also reveal that investors and advisors share many of the same ideas about what makes a good financial partnership.

EQUAL PARTNERSHIP

Eighty-five percent of the women and 83% of the advisors in the survey agree that they must be equal partners in making investment decisions. Both groups, however, agree that the advisor should be responsible for generating most of the investment ideas and explaining how they fit into the investment plan.

STRONG FINANCIAL PLAN

Ninety percent of the women surveyed said that having a structured financial plan in place is important. And by an overwhelming margin, financial advisors agree. Nearly all of the advisors surveyed—97% of them—believe it's important for an advisor to help a client develop a financial plan to meet her long-term goals.

CLEAR EXPLANATIONS

Women and their advisors agree that clear explanations about how specific investments perform and how they fit into a financial plan are critical to making the right decisions. 84% of the women surveyed are happy with the explanations their advisors provide.

RESPECTFUL TREATMENT

Women who aren't treated as serious investors are less likely to establish or maintain relationships with financial professionals. But 97% of the women surveyed said they are pleased with the way they are treated.

As financial advisors and women investors have come to recognize, there are real advantages for both groups in working together.

American women have money to invest. The Bureau of Labor Statistics reports that they earn over $1 trillion annually. They make up 40% of the population with assets over $500,000, much of it inherited from their parents or husbands. Increasingly, they are owners of their own businesses. Yet so far, only a small percentage of women actively invest their money in equities like stocks and mutual funds.

Financial advisors have the expertise women need to make informed decisions.

WINNING COMBINATIONS

As people become increasingly responsible for investing their retirement funds, they need help in choosing the best selections from a constantly expanding marketplace. Most advisors expect that women will make up a larger proportion of investors in the future, and a larger proportion of their client base. While only a third of the advisors in the OppenheimerFunds survey said that they had actively targeted women clients in the past, the majority said that they intend to market to women. In fact, 87% said they expect a larger proportion of women as clients in the future.

Myth #6: If I Invest, My Money Will Be Tied Up

It's a real mistake to think of investing as constraining your financial independence.

Many women believe that if they invest, they'll be tying up their money. But you don't have to settle for smaller returns in order to have easy access to your assets. In fact, you have as much or more **liquidity**, or ability to turn your investments into cash, with mutual funds or most stocks as you do with CDs. That's because if you need money, you can always sell your investments. The risk of course, is that they may have decreased in value.

◀ LESS LIQUID

COLLECTIBLES	REAL ESTATE	STOCKS	BONDS
Things you collect might be worth a great deal of money some day	Over time, real estate generally increases in value, sometimes dramatically	Over time, stocks have provided better returns than other investments	Most bonds offer regular income while you own them, and return your investment when they come due
Collecting is risky because buyers are hard—sometimes impossible—to find if you need to sell	You could have a hard time selling at the price you want, and property may not gain value as it has in the past	Share prices change regularly, so there's always a chance you could lose part or all of your investment	Bond prices vary, so you might have to sell for less than you paid if you need the cash before the investment period ends

YOU CAN'T STAMP OUT INFLATION

Nothing's more liquid than cash. With enough of it in your pocket (or a cash substitute like a check) you can pay for almost anything at all. That's why people like to have it on hand. And it may be one reason they shy away from investments.

But the problem with cash, including the money in regular checking accounts and most savings accounts, is that it doesn't grow. In fact, it actually loses value over time because of the effects of **inflation**, the steady, gradual increase in the cost of nearly everything. The increase in first class postage is just one example.

RISING COST OF POSTAGE

1965	5¢
1968	6¢
1971	8¢
1974	10¢
1975	13¢
1978	15¢
1981	18¢
1981	20¢
1985	22¢
1988	25¢
1991	29¢
1995	32¢

INVESTING YOUR CASH

What should you do if you've got money sitting in a checking or savings account and you want it to be earning more? One solution is to move your money into a range of different investments.

For example, you could put some money in **cash equivalents**, like money market mutual funds. They usually pay more than savings accounts, and

you can access the money easily by check or you can transfer it directly to your bank. But money market funds are not insured and could lose value (see page 83).

You could also buy **U.S. Treasury bills**, or **T-bills** (see page 79). They usually pay more interest than savings accounts and can be sold easily. Better yet, you can buy T-bills for short terms—13 or 26 weeks— so you can time them to come due when you need the money. The minimum investment is $1,000, and you can buy any number of T-bills you want.

Last, but not least, you can invest in mutual funds and stocks, which generally provide significantly better returns than many other investments. You can liquidate them easily at their current value, and, if necessary, you can borrow against certain assets you have in a brokerage account if you need money in a hurry.

MORE LIQUID ▶

CDs	MUTUAL FUNDS	MONEY MARKET FUNDS	CASH
CDs are insured, you know what you'll earn and when the money will be available	Mutual funds offer built-in diversity, management expertise and ease of investing	These mutual funds give you easy access to your money, and interest income	It's readily accessible
Earnings probably won't beat inflation over the long haul and you may owe a penalty for early withdrawal	Earnings and prices aren't guaranteed, so you might sell for less if you had to act quickly	The earnings won't stay ahead of inflation over the long haul, and they're not insured against loss	Cash doesn't grow, so as time passes, it loses value through inflation and may leave you short of funds

SOLID INVESTMENTS

While some investments can be more difficult to liquidate quickly than others—including real estate and certain types of stocks and bonds—they still can be smart places to put your money. That's because their potential advantages more than offset the risks of tying up your capital.

Real estate—land and houses—can increase significantly in value, and may provide you with a place to live or work. There can also be tax advantages to investing in real estate. You may be able to deduct property taxes and interest payments on mortgages and home equity loans.

However, prices tend to move up or down depending on the economy, and on which geographic areas are growing. Those factors can make it hard to predict real estate's long-term performance as an investment.

WORKING THE SYSTEM

One reason all your investments don't have to be liquid is that you can often plan major purchases or postpone expected bills for a time when one of your investments is coming due. For example, you can plan to buy a new car with money from a maturing CD.

Myth #7: I'm Afraid I'll Make Mistakes

The surest way to lose money is to sit on it.

You're not alone if you're afraid of making mistakes with your money. Most people are. And everybody makes a few. But the more you learn about investing, the more you'll realize that the biggest mistake you can make is being too cautious—or worse yet, doing nothing at all.

That's because inflation is the biggest threat to long-term security. It eats away at the value of your **principal**, the money you already have. The only real protection is growth, which increases the size of your portfolio. That way, you'll be able to stay ahead of inflation.

You don't need a lot of money to be an investor. The chart below demonstrates clearly that even small amounts invested regularly can produce real growth. If you invest $50 a month for 25 years and earn 8% a year, you'll more than triple your money.

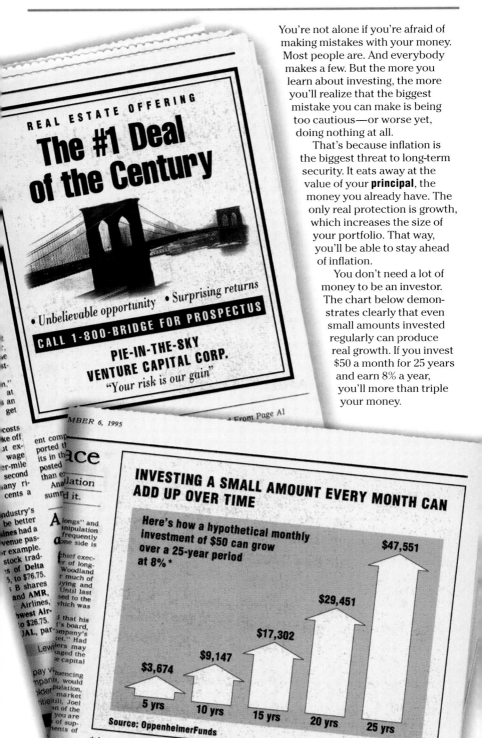

REAL ESTATE OFFERING

The #1 Deal of the Century

- Unbelievable opportunity • Surprising returns

CALL 1-800-BRIDGE FOR PROSPECTUS

PIE-IN-THE-SKY VENTURE CAPITAL CORP.

"Your risk is our gain"

INVESTING A SMALL AMOUNT EVERY MONTH CAN ADD UP OVER TIME

Here's how a hypothetical monthly investment of $50 can grow over a 25-year period at 8% *

- $3,674 — 5 yrs
- $9,147 — 10 yrs
- $17,302 — 15 yrs
- $29,451 — 20 yrs
- $47,551 — 25 yrs

Source: OppenheimerFunds

MEASURING THE ODDS

Risk is the chance you take that your investments will decrease in value instead of making money. You can stress safety by investing in CDs and savings accounts. The problem is, they don't work as long-term investments because they don't grow in value. Or, at the other extreme, you can risk every penny by putting money into a pie-in-the-sky deal that promises great returns and goes bust.

You're better off investing in a solid foundation of mutual funds, stocks and bonds. If your mutual fund earns a little less than the one you didn't buy, it doesn't mean you're doomed to the poor house. And if a stock's performance is lackluster in a dull market, it may turn around when the market rises. You'll be making a more serious mistake if you

panic and sell off your holdings every time the markets decline. As your investments change in price—as they invariably will—you're more likely to come out ahead than someone who thought she was avoiding risk by selling every time the market dropped.

WHO'S TO BLAME?

Some experts suggest that there's a fundamental difference between women investors and their male counterparts. When women lose money they tend to blame themselves. But men often blame the market—or their broker.

THROUGH THICK AND THIN: FOUR BASIC INVESTING RULES

Start

The essence of investing is that money earns money. The sooner the process starts, the more it can earn. That means the biggest mistake you can make as an investor is to wait—especially if you're waiting to find the perfect place to put your money.

A lump sum of $10,000 earning 8% for	Can add up to**
10 years	$21,590
20 years	$46,610
30 years	$100,630

Stick With It

Investments grow best when they are nurtured with regular infusions of new money. That way, you're building the base on which you're earning.

$2,000 invested yearly, earning 8%	Can add up to**
10 years	$31,291
20 years	$98,844
30 years	$244,692

Diversify

If you have all your money in one place, you're much more vulnerable to weak performance than if you invest in a broader range. Any investment can have a poor year, but usually when one is down, others can be doing well enough to offset the loss.

	1980	1985	1990	1995
Large company stocks	↑32%	↑50%	↓10%	↑37%
Corporate bonds	↓3%	↑2%	↑5%	↑27%

Source: Ibbotson Associates

Be Open-Minded

You may be most comfortable keeping most of your money in investments you've always used, like CDs. But by expanding your portfolio to include stocks and mutual funds, you won't risk limiting your earnings when interest rates are low.

	8/84	4/89	2/94	5/96
1-year CDs paid	11.69%	9.49%	3.10%	4.84%

Source: Bank Rate Monitor

The Power of Investing

The more you know about investing, the more confident you'll be about making decisions.

None of the factors that defines you—age, gender, marital status, your education—limits what you can learn or the uses to which you can put your investment knowledge.

The difference between people who make the most of investment opportunities and those who don't isn't necessarily the amount they invest. Most of the time, it's how carefully they plan, how soon they start investing and how consistently they stick with it.

Knowl edge =

PUTTING KNOWLEDGE TO WORK

Learning investing, like learning anything else, works best when you put your knowledge to work right from the start. It might help to compare learning about investing to learning how to handle a job or play a sport. You certainly weren't born with those skills, and chances are you had some help on your way to mastering them. But you did it. The same is true of learning about investing.

The knowledge you need to be an effective investor will come from a combination of the money-management skills you already have, the information you can get in this book and other sources and the help of a financial advisor. Whether you're just starting an investing program or are ready to expand your horizons there are four basic things you need to know:

WHICH investments are available

HOW they work

WHY specific ones will help you meet your goals

WHEN to sell

HERE'S ONE APPROACH YOU MIGHT TRY:

1 When you've finished reading this book, identify one type of investment you want to make—perhaps a mutual fund or stock.

2 Narrow your choice to a specific investment by talking to your financial advisor.

3 Invest in your choice promptly, and add to it regularly .

4 Track how well your investment performs by reading the information you get in the mail, checking its price in the newspapers and asking your advisor for regular updates.

5 After a year, evaluate how well your investment has performed in comparison with similar investments, with how well you expected it to do and with what you had been earning on your money before you invested.

6 If the investment is meeting your objectives, keep building it systematically. If not, consider an alternative investment.

DIFFERENT PATHS

The best way to learn about investing depends a lot on your personality, your life style and your financial goals. That's true whether you pursue the information on your own or with the help of a financial advisor.

If you prefer to develop your investment skills independently, you might take an adult education course at a local school, ask your bank or legal advisor about investment seminars designed for women, or begin reading personal finance columns in the magazines and newspapers you subscribe to.

Whatever your initial approach, you'll probably find it makes sense to work with a professional advisor in developing your investment plan, a subject that's discussed in detail in chapter four.

THE MORE YOU KNOW...

Research conducted by OppenheimerFunds and other groups has found that in the past women have tended to invest too conservatively and therefore less profitably than men. But women who are more confident about their investment knowledge regularly commit more of their income to investing and make more growth-oriented investment choices.

Some of that increased confidence is the product of greater commitment in the financial community to meeting women's needs. Some of it results from the growing experience of women in the workforce, and some from a widespread sense that in the future government help for people who are retiring will be scaled back.

Whatever the reasons, the resulting financial security women can create for themselves should make a major difference in their lives. At the very least, it can reduce the fear many women have of ending up as a burden to their children if they can't afford to live independently when they are older.

Investing can—and often does—mean the difference between realizing your goals and having to settle for less.

Investing rewards the people who make choices best suited to meeting their personal goals.

Successful investing is within everyone's grasp.

DJIA

SHOULD YOU KNOW WHERE THE MARKET IS TODAY?

If you can't quote the Dow Jones Industrial Average, the best-known stock market index, or aren't sure whether it's up or down, should you abandon any thought of investing? Of course not—any more than you'd abandon a trip you've planned to a special destination because you haven't tracked the average temperature there.

The DJIA and other stock market indexes do help you follow what other investors are doing. But despite the attention the Dow gets, following its gyrations isn't what makes a successful investor. Knowing where your money is, why it's there, and how it's doing are far more important.

Investing on Your Own

Being single isn't one category—it's many different ones.

As a woman, there's a 90% chance that you're responsible for managing your own financial affairs now or will be someday. Whether you find the idea exciting or frightening, the likelihood of managing your money means you'll need to know as much as you can, not only about your day-to-day expenses but about investing. This knowledge will not only help you keep your head above water, but it will also make it possible to realize your personal financial goals.

INVESTING FOR ONE

There's no one right way for a single woman to invest. (Single includes those who never marry, those who divorce and those who are widowed. It also includes those who are heads of households, who live with partners, or who live alone.) Your age will make a difference as well, since the period of time you have to invest for specific goals will affect the investment strategies you use. For example, a woman in her 20s and a woman in her 60s might both be investing for retirement. The former is likely to look for investments that will grow in value, while the latter may be shifting to investments that produce income.

SINGLE

If you are single and have no dependents, you may not be responsible for other people's welfare. If you don't have to worry about providing health care for your parents, paying for a college education, or making sure your spouse has enough to live on after you die, you can invest for the things you value for yourself.

At the same time, you are the only one responsible for your financial security. Most women who collect Social Security based on their own earnings collect less than men and less than widows. That makes it doubly important to invest through employer-sponsored retirement plans or set up your own tax-deferred account if you're self-employed.

WHAT THE NUMBERS SHOW BY AGE GROUP

	20s
NEVER MARRIED	35.3%
MARRIED	52.8%
DIVORCED	6.8%
WIDOWED	.03%

Source: U.S. Bureau of the Census, 1994

FINDING HELP

If you find that investment information that's generally available seems designed for a traditional couple, don't despair. You can get investment information that's tailored for you.

- Look for a financial advisor who has experience working with single women

- Find an investment discussion group or seminar that's designed for singles. Check with your local library, civic center, religious or educational institution

- Get information from your professional or union affiliation

- Find out about an existing investment club you can join, or discuss forming one with your friends and colleagues (see page 16)

- Contact local or national women's groups for information and referrals. The Older Women's League is just one example. You can call them at 202-783-6686, or write to 666 11th Street, NW, Suite 700, Washington, D.C. 20001

FAMILY HEAD

If you're a single woman with children, you are responsible for their well-being as well as your own. In fact, you may have put your own long-term goals on hold to meet your children's needs.

No one can fault you for that. But you should also be looking for ways to invest for your future, even while your current invest-ments are helping to pay for your children's education. You're likely to live a lot longer after they're on their own.

One good way to build your nest egg while meeting other expenses is by putting money into a retirement plan sponsored by your employer (see pages 130–131). These plans have the added benefit of reducing your current taxes and providing a source for loans should you need some cash in the short term.

NEWLY SINGLE

If you suddenly find yourself single and responsible for your own finances after many years of marriage, your primary concern may well be making the money you have last as long as you'll need it. And if you've never been involved in investment decisions, the responsibility may seem overwhelming.

But it doesn't have to be, because you can get the help you need to make wise decisions. Attorneys who specialize in Elder Law, for example, do much of their work for women. If you don't have a financial advisor, or are uncomfortable working with the one your husband used, ask your lawyer about finding someone to work with. Or, you can ask for advice and professional referrals from your children or from other relatives or friends who have had similar experiences.

30s	40–54	55–65	65–74	75–84	85 and over
12.8%	5.9%	4.1%	3.8%	4.0%	8.0%
66.7%	68.3%	66.1%	52.4%	30.3%	13.3%
14.1%	16.6%	12.6%	7.7%	4.1%	2.9%
1.20%	4.7%	13.9%	34.2%	59.9%	73.7%

Table does not include married women living apart from their husbands.

EMERGENCY FUNDS

Financial emergencies happen in every-body's life, whether you're single or married. The real issues aren't whether, or even when, they will happen, but how they can be resolved.

One safety net that most financial experts recommend is an **emergency fund**, money set aside in an account you can tap easily—like your bank or mutual fund money market account (though not your checking account), or in short-term investments like Certificates of Deposit (CDs) or U.S. Treasury bills.

You'll find that different financial experts suggest different reserve amounts, with the most typical being the equivalent of three to six months salary. Experts differ dramatically, though, on how much a *single* woman should keep in reserve.

Some advisors, who recognize the consequences of keeping too much money in low-paying accounts, urge women to invest most of their emergency money in a balanced portfolio of stocks, bonds and mutual funds. The argument is that you can always sell the investments if you must have the cash. It is possible that you might lose some money if you need to sell on short notice, but the odds that you'll come out ahead are statistically in your favor.

Other advisors, who are concerned that women on their own may have more difficulty getting assistance from their families or a harder time finding a new job, think that women should keep more money in emergency funds than the amount they recommend for men.

While you'll have to make the final decision about the size of your reserve fund, you should resist the temptation to confuse being cautious with dragging your heels about putting your money to work.

Married, with Investments

Investing to meet your shared goals can forge a special bond between you and your husband.

Investing together may not strike you as especially romantic, but it can be a very satisfying part of marriage, something that you can do, and benefit from, together. Even more important, there's such strong evidence that women should be active investors that ignoring the opportunity to build those skills together simply defies logic.

Sharing investment decisions may come about naturally if you handle the other parts of your financial life together. But if you've done things more traditionally, with your husband making all the investment decisions, you may need to exert some effort to change the pattern.

A MARRIAGE BONUS

Marriage has lots of benefits, financially speaking. Consider just a few.

Accumulating Capital

As a married couple committed to investing, you have some

Diversifying Your Portfolios

It can be easier for a married couple to follow some of the basic principles of investing,

Planning Your Estate

As a married couple you can benefit from estate planning, especially if you invest success-fully. Since *each* person can give

OUTSIDE INFLUENCES

If you and your husband have been postponing working together on investment decisions, other people's experiences can jar you into action—or encourage one of you to press for change.

For example, you may have a close friend who made decisions she later regretted because she was uncomfortable handling investments. Or you may have tried to help a relative cope not only with the grief of widowhood but the trauma of sudden financial responsibility.

Here's one schedule for getting started:

● Talk with your husband about the financial goals you share

● Discuss what you've done to help make them realities

● Make a list of your investment questions

● Find a financial advisor to help provide answers and plan future investments

● Review all your investment decisions together on a regular schedule

MINE, YOURS OR OURS

Investing together doesn't mean you can't also invest separately, especially if you have some very different priorities. For example, you can decide how to invest money you put into retirement plans at work or into Individual Retirement Accounts (IRAs).

Money or investments you inherit are also yours, as are investments you owned before you got married. You can continue to hold them separately, or share ownership with your husband. It's probably smart to discuss the alternatives—and their legal and tax consequences—with him, your family and your lawyer.

advantages in accumulating the money you need and putting it to work for you.

While it may not be true that two can live as cheaply as one, you can certainly live more cheaply together than you could apart, leaving the balance for investment. As the traditional family expands to include more women who work outside the home, you may have more income to invest plus the added benefit of two tax-deferred retirement plans to which you can contribute regularly.

such as **diversification**. The whole notion of diversification is owning various types of investments that perform differently (see pages 100–101). But the problem often is having enough money to do it.

If you have two incomes, you can buy a diverse mix of investments for each of your retirement and regular investment accounts. Or better yet you can work together to diversify your overall investments. One of the advantages of planning your investments across the board is that you have a lot more flexibility in getting the diversification you want.

away or leave property tax-free, up to $650,000 in 1999 (increasing to $1 million in 2006), it makes sense for couples with substantial assets, or assets they expect to increase, to divide up ownership of their property—effectively doubling the amount they can leave tax-free.

There's no cap on the value of property husbands and wives can give each other without owing gift tax, so you can split your assets evenly even if one of you paid most of the expense of buying them. You will reduce the taxes your estate might eventually owe, while leaving whichever of you lives longer adequate income. Since estate planning and related tax issues are complicated, be sure to work with a tax attorney on this part of your investment plan.

WORKING WITH AN ADVISOR

If your investment partnership is going to be effective, you and your husband must both be comfortable working with your financial advisor. One of you may already have a working relationship that can be expanded to include a third person. If the three of you can consult as equals, it probably makes good sense to build on the existing association.

If either you or your husband is treated like a third wheel or feels ignored, however, it probably makes sense to look for a new advisor together. You both may be more comfortable asking questions or expressing opinions if you're starting with a clean slate.

You and your husband can make your partnership approach clear if you both participate in the conversation, both ask questions and consult with each other, instead of having one of you seem to be making all the decisions.

Some Details of Ownership

There's more to owning property than simply knowing where to sign your name.

You can own investments several different ways. If you buy a mutual fund, for instance, you can own it in your own name, jointly with one or more other people, or as a trustee for the benefit of someone else.

In each case, the way you own an investment determines your rights as an owner, including whether you can sell the property or give it to someone else. Your parents, for example, could give property to you and your siblings in equal shares, allowing each of you the right to sell your shares separately. Or they could make it a requirement that you all agree before any part of it could be sold.

KINDS OF OWNERSHIP

Basically, there are four ways to own property, whether it's real estate (land and buildings), stocks, bonds, mutual funds, bank accounts or almost anything else:

	SOLE OWNERSHIP	JOINT TENANTS WITH RIGHTS OF SURVIVORSHIP
Owners	One person owns the property and controls what happens to it.	Two (or potentially more than two) people own the property equally.
Right to sell	There are no limits on selling it, giving it away or leaving it by will as long as you own the property outright.	One person can sell his or her share, but usually only with the consent of the other owner(s) and only if the proceeds of the sale are shared equally with the other owner(s).
In a divorce	Property purchased during a marriage could be counted as marital property that's subject to division.	If the owners are a married couple, and they divorce, the property is included in the marital property that's subject to division.
At death	Property can be left by will or trust as the owner wishes.	When one owner dies, that share immediately becomes the property of the other owner(s).

YOU DON'T ALWAYS GET IT IN WRITING
When you buy certain property, like a car or real estate, you get a title, or certificate of ownership, that names you as the owner. It must be signed over to the new owner when you sell. In fact, the process of finalizing ownership is often referred to as **taking title**.

In the past, you also used to get certificates when you bought stocks and bonds, which you had to safeguard and then sign and turn in when you wanted to sell. But when you buy securities today, ownership is recorded in book-entry form. You can usually sell securities simply by giving instructions over the phone and having the money transferred to your account.

ACHING JOINTS
Joint ownership won't always protect you from having the rug pulled out from under you, financially speaking. When you have joint checking or savings accounts, or any account that doesn't require both signatures to transfer or withdraw money, either owner can take out every penny, perfectly legally.

FLEXIBLE OWNERSHIP

Ownership can be changed, often relatively simply. If you want to make your husband, your adult child or some other person a joint owner of property that you now own alone, you can usually change the title with little hassle and rarely any expense. With a mutual fund account, for example, you write a letter of instruction to the custodian. With a stock certificate, you complete the transfer section on the back. In either case, you might have to get a signature guarantee from your bank.

With joint ownership, you and the other owner(s) have to agree before a change can be made. But if you do, you can make whatever changes you want, even if the sole purpose is to save you money on taxes.

However, you should avoid acting too hastily. For example, lawyers often advise newly married people to keep assets they had before marriage in their own names, at least for a time. If you live in a **community property state** (see page 142), in fact, you may decide to hold premarital property in sole ownership no matter how long you're married. Otherwise, you give up your right to own it exclusively in the future.

TENANTS BY THE ENTIRETY	TENANTS IN COMMON
This must be a married couple who own the property together.	Two or more people own a share—generally an equal share—of the property.
Neither can sell without the other's permission.	Each owner can sell his or her share independently and keep all the profit. The other owner(s) have no right to inherit (though they could), and they have no control over what happens to a co-owner's share.
Spouses become tenants in common. Either has the right to sell his or her half without the consent of the other.	Property purchased during a marriage could be counted as marital property that's subject to division.
When one spouse dies, the other becomes the sole owner of the property.	Property can be left by will or trust as the owner wishes.

GETTING ADVICE

If you're married or involved in a long-term partnership, you should discuss ownership decisions with your lawyer and probably with your tax advisor.

Many married couples own all their investments, including their homes, jointly. There are good reasons for this, including the fact that it helps to establish financial equity between husband and wife and may prevent one partner—for whatever reason—from selling all the assets. But there are potential drawbacks to owning everything jointly, including protecting assets from federal estate taxes or claims from your or your husband's creditors.

Though you can't prepare for every eventuality, your lawyer might advise you to limit joint ownership if one of you might be vulnerable to lawsuits because of your profession or other activities. Trying to shift ownership in the face of a legal threat usually doesn't work.

WHEN TIME COUNTS

One caution: there are times when a transfer of ownership might be challenged in court, usually in cases when you're trying to protect certain assets or qualify for government assistance. In those cases, transfers have to occur before a specific date—sometimes as long as three years or more—to be valid.

Investing with a Partner

When the tie that binds you is not marriage, investing together can be a bit more complex.

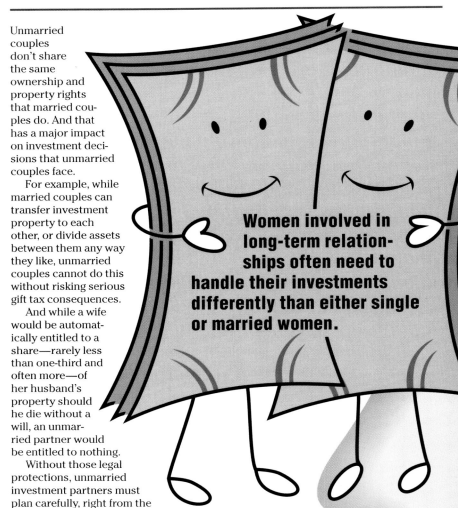

Unmarried couples don't share the same ownership and property rights that married couples do. And that has a major impact on investment decisions that unmarried couples face.

For example, while married couples can transfer investment property to each other, or divide assets between them any way they like, unmarried couples cannot do this without risking serious gift tax consequences.

And while a wife would be automatically entitled to a share—rarely less than one-third and often more—of her husband's property should he die without a will, an unmarried partner would be entitled to nothing.

Without those legal protections, unmarried investment partners must plan carefully, right from the beginning, for equitable ways to own and distribute their property, not only in case of separation, but also when one of them dies.

Women involved in long-term relationships often need to handle their investments differently than either single or married women.

The annual ceiling on tax-free gifts applies to property transfers between unmarried partners.

If your partner dies without a will, you may not have a legal right to property held in his or her name.

Older couples may choose not to marry to make it easier to leave their entire estates to children from earlier marriages.

SHARING THE WEALTH

JOINT OWNERSHIP

With the exception of the arrangement known as tenants by the entirety(see page 31), unmarried partners can own investment assets any way they choose: solely, jointly or as tenants in common. Joint tenancy works the same way for unmarried as for married people. At the death of one owner, the property automatically goes to the survivor.

However, when a couple is unmarried, the total value of the property is legally considered part of the estate of the first to die. That could mean higher estate and inheritance taxes for the remaining unmarried partner because while a surviving spouse who is a U.S. citizen can inherit any amount without owing federal estate taxes, unmarried partners can not.

NAMING BENEFICIARIES

If you name your partner as beneficiary for your pension, retirement plan or insurance policy, that person will collect the money the plan provides when you die.

Your partner won't have the same right your husband would to roll over any retirement payout into a tax-deferred IRA, but you will have insured that the money goes to the right person. An added advantage is that documents naming beneficiaries are less likely to be contested than wills.

CREATING TRUSTS

Another way to pass investment assets to your partner outside your will is to create a **trust,** a legal document that transfers ownership to a trustee until it goes to the beneficiary either at your death or at any time you name. Of course, there are many other uses for trusts. Married couples use trusts for tax-saving reasons as well as naming beneficiaries and controlling how the assets are spent. Many people who own property in more than one state or want to leave assets to minors prefer trusts to wills.

You shouldn't attempt to create trusts without legal advice, though. They must be drawn up correctly to achieve the results you want.

IN TRUST FOR...

You can arrange to leave money directly to a specific person when you die, without the expense of establishing a formal trust agreement or including the bequest in your will. You can set up a Totten Trust, a bank account **in trust for** the person you want to have it. Or you may be able to set up Transfer on Death (TOD) registration for your mutual fund accounts. At your death, the beneficiary you've named becomes the owner. But at any time before you die, you can change your mind about any aspect of the bequest, take the money out, or add assets to the account.

It's always best to get legal advice about any arrangements you make to dispose of your property. That's especially true if you're concerned that your family might contest bequests you make to your partner.

BUYING AN ANNUITY

Annuities, or investments you make now to provide income later, are another way to provide financial security for your unmarried partner, especially one who seems likely to outlive you.

Basically, you invest in the annuity, either in a lump sum or over a period of years, naming your partner as beneficiary or co-beneficiary with yourself. At a date you select, the annuity begins to pay out the accumulating assets of your investment, providing an income for life or for a set period of years. Here, as with other assets that are transferred outside a will, there is less risk of legal challenge.

You and your partner may have more trouble arranging for a mortgage than a married couple with comparable income.

IF THE SHOE FITS

All the techniques described on these pages as ways of transferring investment assets to an unmarried partner work similarly if you use them on behalf of your husband, children, family or friends. (Remember, though, you have to make special arrangements for children who are minors.)

Except for certain trust documents, most of these techniques are **revocable**, which means you maintain control of the assets while you are alive, and you can change the beneficiary. Yet all of them are designed to let you pass along assets with less time, trouble and expense and, if it's important to you, with less publicity than though a will.

Financial Planning

A strong financial future begins with a sound financial plan.

Maybe you're just starting your career. Perhaps you've already retired. Or maybe you're somewhere in between. Whatever your situation, you probably have some specific financial goals. But you may be uncertain of the best way to reach them. Or you may wonder how to achieve your more immediate goals without losing sight of those down the road. What you need is a financial plan.

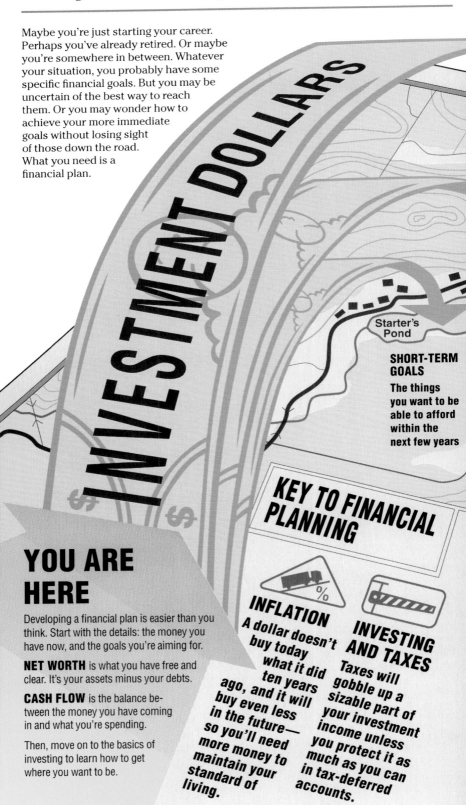

INVESTMENT DOLLARS

Starter's Pond

SHORT-TERM GOALS

The things you want to be able to afford within the next few years

KEY TO FINANCIAL PLANNING

YOU ARE HERE

Developing a financial plan is easier than you think. Start with the details: the money you have now, and the goals you're aiming for.

NET WORTH is what you have free and clear. It's your assets minus your debts.

CASH FLOW is the balance between the money you have coming in and what you're spending.

Then, move on to the basics of investing to learn how to get where you want to be.

INFLATION
A dollar doesn't buy today what it did ten years ago, and it will buy even less in the future—so you'll need more money to maintain your standard of living.

INVESTING AND TAXES
Taxes will gobble up a sizable part of your investment income unless you protect it as much as you can in tax-deferred accounts.

NO SILENT PARTNERS

Since the whole point of financial planning is finding ways to meet your goals, you need to know what's important to *you*, and how *you* plan to achieve it. Then, if you are working with a husband or a partner, you'll be ready to put your ideas together.

If asserting yourself about family finances is hard for you, especially when you try to talk about planning, then it's worth the extra effort. You'll probably find that the more you know about investing the easier the conversation will become.

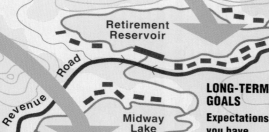

Retirement Reservoir

Road

Revenue

Midway Lake

FINANCIAL HEIGHTS

LONG-TERM GOALS

Expectations you have for later on, including a comfortable retirement and something to leave your heirs

MID-TERM GOALS

The hopes and plans you have for big-ticket items farther down the road

HIDDEN ASSETS

Many people think the ideal approach to financial planning is a cooperative effort, with husbands and wives making decisions together. Nevertheless, 13% of the women in a 1995 Working Woman survey said they had separate accounts that they kept secret from their husbands. They gave several reasons, from being ready for emergencies to investing for personal goals.

INVESTING FOR GROWTH

Investments that grow in value can help you achieve your long-term goals by building your net worth.

CHOOSING INVESTMENTS

A financial plan can help you identify investments that are well-suited to achieving your goals.

**FIVE STEPS
TO CREATING
A FINANCIAL
PLAN**

#1

Taking a Closer Look

Doing financial planning helps you focus
on your goals.

If there are things about your
financial situation that are
hard to face, avoiding them
won't help. Before you can
plan for the future, you have to take a
hard look at your current finances,
including your salary and other income,
and your spending habits.

FOCUS ON YOUR BUDGET

Just thinking **budget** may send a shiver up your spine. But *budget* isn't an
order to tighten up. It's a statement of the money you have coming in and
the places you're spending it. If you want to save or invest more, but stay
within your budget, you can increase your income or reduce your expenses.
The first may be better, but the second can actually be easier. Here's what
a typical budget might look like for someone earning $48,000 a year.

MONTHLY INCOME		MONTHLY EXPENSES	
Salary	$ 3,900	Housing	$ 1,100
Interest and dividends	100	Food	600
		Miscellaneous	200
		Entertainment	150
		Transportation	200
		Medical care	100
		Credit card bills	250
		Income Tax	1,000
		Investments	400
TOTAL MONTHLY INCOME	**$ 4,000**	**TOTAL MONTHLY EXPENSES**	**$ 4,000**

If your total income is more than your expenses, you can afford to build your investment accounts.

Reduce the cost of your debt by paying off credit cards that charge high interest rates.

Your goal should be to put at least 10% of your income into your investment accounts.

FIGURING NET WORTH

The other thing you need to know before creating a financial plan is your **net worth**, which is the difference between your **assets**, or what you have, and your **liabilities**, or what you owe.

You can get a sense of how you've done so far in building your financial security by figuring your net worth.

**ASSETS
– LIABILITIES
= NET WORTH**

ADD ASSETS

$ **Cash**

$ **Savings**

$ **Investments**

$ **Your home (if you own it)**

$ **Your personal property**

$ **Money people owe you**

SUBTRACT LIABILITIES

$ **Mortgage or rent**

$ **Loans and unpaid bills**

$ **Insurance due**

$ **This month's credit card totals**

$ **Any taxes you owe**

Your net worth constantly fluctuates, as the market value of your assets and the amount of your debt changes.

$

TRACKING EXPENSES

Taking a hard look at your expenses may not be much fun, but it can help you understand why you're having a hard time investing as much of your income as you'd like.

One approach is to keep track—dollar by dollar—of what you spend in a month, or better yet, over several months. Even if you forget a few major expenses, you'll get a good idea of your financial situation.

Keeping track of your expenses doesn't have to be a guilt trip. But knowing where the money's going can help you decide what's really worth the price, and where you can cut back most easily. There are many good software packages that can help.

You can find ways to cut back on what you spend every day by buying more carefully.

FIVE STEPS
TO CREATING
A FINANCIAL
PLAN

#2

Creating a Plan

Required equipment: a sharp pencil, an eraser, blank paper.

Getting your goals down in black and white helps you focus on what's really important to you. Nothing is too trivial or too fantastic, at least in the initial planning stages. And creating the list will probably help you clarify your priorities.

DEFINING FINANCIAL PLANS

It's easy to get confused about what a financial plan is because the same term is used to mean different things.

Very simply, your **financial plan** is an informal list of the things you'd like to be able to afford in the future, and the steps you'll take to obtain them.

A financial plan can also refer to a formal document prepared by a financial advisor that provides an analysis of your current financial situation, explains financial planning strategies and identifies specific investments.

All financial plans—informal and formal—come to the same conclusion: the difference between keeping your head above water and investing toward your dreams is how much, how well and how soon you invest.

PHONY SAVINGS PLANS

Remember, there's a difference between saving and investing. Be sure to distinguish between making real investments and simply saving more. If your nest egg isn't growing and earning money, you're not making progress toward meeting your future goals.

Among the worst choices: holiday or vacation clubs that pay no interest, and deliberately planned income tax refunds. That's because all you get back is what you put in. You'd get the same results stuffing the money in a mattress.

Instead, you can find ways to invest at the same pace you would with these less productive plans, perhaps by having part of your paycheck direct-deposited into a mutual fund, or having a specific amount transferred regularly from your checking account. You can invest in U.S. Savings Bonds directly too, but you have to hold each one for its entire term to collect its full face value.

FINANCIAL PLANNING WORKSHEET

Short-Term Goals

Make specific investing decisions for the next few years

Mid-Term Goals

Sketch the major expenses you visualize for the next ten years

Retirement Goals

Commit a percentage of your income to tax-deferred investments and let them grow

KEEPING YOUR PLAN ON TRACK

Financial planning is an on going process. First of all, you have to put your plan into action by investing regularly. For example, if you commit yourself to adding $2,000 a year to your IRA (Individual Retirement Account), it's easier to contribute $166 a month than to come up with the entire

INVEST IN YOURSELF

To build a strong enough financial base you'll need two things: money and time.

Sometimes, though, you may have financial opportunities, like buying a home or building up a business, before you have enough cash to afford the investment.

That's why financial plans often include borrowing to meet your more immediate goals. You can think about paying off these loans as the equivalent of putting money into an investment account—except you're already enjoying the benefits. The only caution is that you should also be investing to meet future goals.

TYPICAL GOALS	POTENTIAL CHOICES
New car	☐ Treasury bills
Down payment on home	☐ CDs
Extra education	☐ Money-market funds
Establishing a business	☐ Short-term bonds
	☐ Balanced funds

TYPICAL GOALS	POTENTIAL CHOICES
Education for children	☐ High-rated bonds or bond funds
Larger home	☐ Stock in well-established companies
Second home	☐ Stock mutual funds
Travel	☐ Treasury notes
	☐ Zero-coupon bonds

TYPICAL GOALS	POTENTIAL CHOICES
Affording travel, hobbies	☐ Growth stocks
Maintaining life style	☐ Stock mutual funds
Security for long-term care	☐ High-interest bonds
Helping children	☐ Long-term bonds
Inheritance for heirs	☐ Zero-coupon bonds

EXPANDING HORIZONS

One of the most exciting and rewarding elements of investing is that you can learn and hopefully earn as you go along. You don't have to pass any tests to start, and you can get instant feedback on how well you're doing.

As with other learning experiences, you'll probably find that success brings added confidence. And you'll be encouraged to expand into new investment areas that offer increased earning potential without greatly increasing your risk.

amount at one time. And since IRAs have an investing deadline (April 15), you risk missing this opportunity entirely if you don't have the money on hand. And remember, the earlier you invest, the more time your money has to grow.

Every year you should also revise and update your financial plan and the investment strategy you're following. For one thing, you probably won't have exactly the same goals today that you had a couple of years ago, or that you will have a couple of years from now.

What's more, investments change in value, depending on what's happening in the economy, within a certain industry, or with a particular mutual fund. You'll want to adjust your plan to take advantage of those changes.

NAME

DATE

Getting the Money Together

Accumulating and allocating investment funds is a key part of your plan.

With your financial plan in hand, you can turn your attention to getting the money together to make the first investment, and the next one and the ones after that.

You don't need much money to open an investment account. And once it's opened you can add to it easily, often as little as $25 at a time. You can have money directly deposited from your pay check or transferred from your checking account, or write a check yourself. The sooner you start and the more regularly you add, the faster the account will grow.

You can also accumulate money in a savings account. But you should compare what you'd earn there with what you're likely to earn by investing right from the start. You may find investing makes more sense for no more effort.

KEEP IT SEPARATE

If you're building an investment account, it makes a lot of sense to keep it separate from your checking account. It will pay off—even if it means another piece of paper to keep track of—because you won't be as tempted to spend your investment money on everyday expenses.

NEW MONEY should be added regularly to investment accounts

INVESTMENT ACCOUNTS

	MUTUAL FUND	BANK MONEY MARKET ACCOUNT	BROKERAGE ACCOUNT
Minimum opening deposit	From $25 to $3,000 or more to start; each fund sets its own initial minimum	Range upward from $1,000; each bank sets its own minimum	From a low of $500 to several thousand dollars, at discretion of firm
Minimum balance	May charge a fee for accounts with balances below initial minimum	May earn less or no interest if balance dips too low	Depends on the account
Costs and fees	Fund expenses such as management fees and sometimes account expenses such as sales fees, or load	May charge fees if balance dips below minimum	Similar to fees for money market account; may be annual fee for cash management
Average return	Mutual fund return reflects stock/bond performance	In 1996, 2.8% was typical, but it could be more or less	Similar to mutual-fund money-market account
Advantages	Diversification, management expertise	Check writing; easy access to money	Easy to invest; many bank-like services available

REINVESTING YOUR EARNINGS

One of the most reliable ways to build your assets is to reinvest the money you earn from the investments you already have. You can do that directly and easily with all mutual funds and some stocks because the company will handle the transaction. All you have to do is participate in the company's reinvestment plan.

With bonds and some stocks, the interest or dividends you earn is paid to you (or your brokerage account) directly, and you have to decide how to invest it. That's where having a financial plan can make a big difference: if you know what you want to do next, you can act promptly—for example, putting the earnings into an investment account where you hope they will generate earnings to help you accumulate money for a bigger purchase.

INVESTMENTS
are purchased with the funds you accumulate

MUTUAL FUNDS

Once you've made an initial investment in a fund, you can add to it any time you have the minimum amount, usually $25 to $100. From more than 7,000 funds available, you can choose stock or bond funds in tune with your goals, which may range from current income to long-term growth.

STOCKS

You can buy stock through a broker or, in some cases, directly from the company. Prices range from less than $1 to more than $100 a share. You can sell stocks you have to buy others. Stocks may provide growth, income or both.

BONDS

Bonds generally cost $1,000 each and may require a minimum purchase of $10,000 or more. Once you have invested, you can use money from maturing bonds to buy new ones. Bonds generally emphasize income, not growth.

CDS

You can open a CD with as little as $250 and earn a guaranteed rate of interest. You can invest for periods of six months to five years, and decide either to withdraw your money at the end of the term or reinvest. CDs are income, not growth, investments.

THE ACCUMULATION PHASE

You can build an investment account from money you're earning by adding a certain amount every paycheck, or every month.

If you stick to the guideline of investing 10% of your annual salary, you're talking about $166 a month if you're earning $20,000 a year, and $833 a month if you're earning $100,000 a year. You can find the monthly amount you're aiming for by dividing your annual salary by 12 and multiplying by 10%.*

If you don't have a steady income, and you're building your investment assets in bursts rather than in regular installments, there's an added incentive for using an account that puts your money directly into investments.

IT'S NOT PIN MONEY ANYMORE

A woman's right to control money of her own has a long history, though in the past it rarely made her financially secure. Cash, commonly known as **pin money**, was allocated for her incidental expenses by a marriage contract. In the original Greek, the term was *paraphernalia*, or things outside the dowry. And in the U.S., where dowries were not the norm, farm women traditionally controlled their **butter and egg money**, or what they earned selling the products they gathered or made.

EARNINGS
can be reinvested

Building Your Portfolio

As you increase the number and variety of your investments, you're also building your confidence as an investor.

You begin to create a **portfolio**, or collection of investments, the moment you open your first mutual fund account or buy your first stock or bond. If you add investment money regularly, you'll build the value of your portfolio over time. That will help put your goals within reach, and it also means you'll be able to diversify your holdings to take advantage of different ways of making money.

Since the process of choosing investments involves learning how the different types perform and what they can contribute to your financial plan, you're building your knowledge along with your assets. The more you know, the more confident you're likely to be in making selections and deciding how to **allocate**, or divide up, the total value of your assets among various investments.

INVESTMENT STYLES
The essence of investing is putting your money to work so you can earn more money with what you already have. You can invest **conservatively**, which means there's little chance you'll lose what you already have, though you'll make less than with the other alternatives. You can invest **moderately**, which means you could come out with substantially more than you started with, but could possibly lose some of your investment. Or you can invest **aggressively**, which means you could make a bundle, but could also have big losses.

Or you can do a little of each.

HOW A PORTFOLIO GROWS

EXTENSIVE PORTFOLIO

Some investors may have significant assets but no financial experience. Women who are widowed, for example, may need to make decisions about investment portfolios their husbands have built.

MID-SIZED PORTFOLIO

SMALL PORTFOLIO

You can start out with just one or two investments.

NOVICE INVESTOR

If you're at the beginning of the investor learning curve or just starting your career as an investor, you may want to move slowly. Whether you're investing money you're accumulating yourself, or a lump sum you've just received, it's time to begin building your assets. Most advisors suggest buying mutual funds.

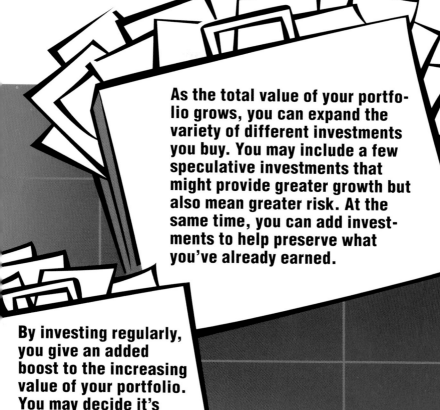

As the total value of your portfolio grows, you can expand the variety of different investments you buy. You may include a few speculative investments that might provide greater growth but also mean greater risk. At the same time, you can add investments to help preserve what you've already earned.

By investing regularly, you give an added boost to the increasing value of your portfolio. You may decide it's time to move into other investments, including those in international markets.

Some investors begin to develop their financial plan before they have much money to invest. But even small amounts can grow into sizable portfolios, especially if you add money regularly.

INTERMEDIATE INVESTOR

With your assets and your investing experience growing, you may be ready to make purchases that require larger sums of money. It's also time to work toward a balanced portfolio that includes a variety of different mutual funds, plus stocks and bonds. You may be developing your own investment style, too, that reflects your time frame and your tolerance for risk.

EXPERIENCED INVESTOR

The more you know about investing, the greater the challenge—and the fun—of choosing where to put your money. And the more money you have to invest, the more diversity you can achieve. With a secure base, you may be ready to try more speculative investments, although the core of your portfolio will continue to be a balance of stocks, bonds and mutual funds.

Choosing Growth or Income

Growth means increasing value, and income means money coming in.

Growth Investments

You buy a **growth investment** anticipating that it will increase in value over time, though there's no way to predict the rate of growth or the change in value. Shares of stock, shares in a mutual fund and real estate (land and the buildings on it), are typical growth investments.

An investment grows in value when its price increases, and you can sell it for more than you paid for it. For example, if you buy 100 shares of stock at $10 a share, and its price goes up to $30 a share, you triple your money on the growth in value.* The difference between the price you paid ($1,000) and the price you sold for ($3,000) is your **capital gain**. In this case, it's $2,000.

BUY

100 shares of stock at $10 per share

$1,000

Year 1   Year 2

Income Investments

Income investments usually pay interest or dividends, depending on the kind of investment they are.

Interest is a percentage of the price of the investment. For example, if you buy a $1,000 bond that's paying 6% interest, you earn $1,000 x .06, or $60 a year.* Investments that pay interest are known as **fixed-income investments**, and include bonds, certificates of deposit and similar investments.

Dividends are part of a company's earnings, divided among its stockholders. For example, if a company paid a $1.50 annual dividend on each share of its stock, and you owned 300 shares, your income would be $450.*

BUY

$1,000 bond at issue paying 6% interest and hold to maturity

$1,000 $60 $60

PAR VALUE OF BOND

The price of a bond, called its **par value**, is usually $1,000 at issue and at redemption

Which to Choose

How can you decide between growth and income investments? Here are some things to consider, based on advice from investment experts:

SUIT YOUR CHOICE TO YOUR GOALS

The longer your time frame, the more sense growth makes, since you can ride out possible downturns in the value of your investment.

The whole point of investing is making money. That happens whether an investment grows in value or pays you income. But while growth and income may seem like equally appealing ideas, they aren't interchangeable goals.

Lots of times, though, you can have it both ways, profiting from growth *and* income. Unlike growth companies that pour their profits back into the business, growth and income investments—usually in older and better established corporations—offer steady, if slower, growth combined with dividends.

The same combination of investment goals is available with some mutual funds, including growth and income, equity-income, balanced and total return funds.

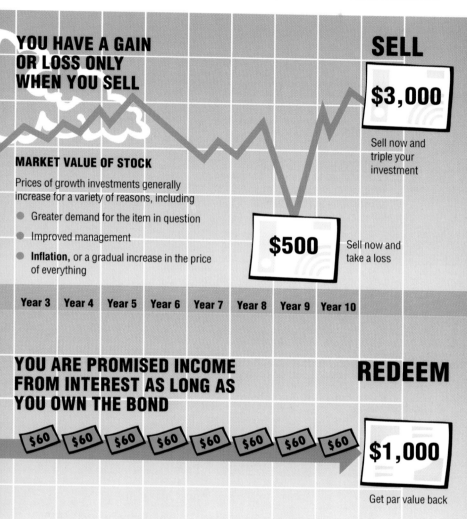

YOU HAVE A GAIN OR LOSS ONLY WHEN YOU SELL

SELL

$3,000

Sell now and triple your investment

MARKET VALUE OF STOCK

Prices of growth investments generally increase for a variety of reasons, including

- Greater demand for the item in question
- Improved management
- **Inflation,** or a gradual increase in the price of everything

$500

Sell now and take a loss

| Year 3 | Year 4 | Year 5 | Year 6 | Year 7 | Year 8 | Year 9 | Year 10 |

YOU ARE PROMISED INCOME FROM INTEREST AS LONG AS YOU OWN THE BOND

REDEEM

$60 $60 $60 $60 $60 $60 $60 $60

$1,000

Get par value back

CONSIDER THE TAX IMPLICATIONS

You can buy income investments for your retirement-plan accounts but postpone paying taxes on those earnings until you withdraw them.

BALANCE YOUR RISK

If you have a variety of investments, you aren't as vulnerable to the economic ups and downs that are sure to come.

MONITOR YOUR INVESTMENTS

As your financial situation changes, be prepared to adjust your investments to switch the focus from growth to income, or vice versa.

Keeping Ahead of Inflation

You have to be prepared for costs that keep going up.

If your investments are going to help you achieve your financial goals, they have to beat **inflation**, the steady increase in the cost of everything.

FINANCIAL FACTS OF LIFE

The truth about inflation is that you need more money every year to pay for the same things. And while you're probably resigned to increases in the cost of dry cleaning, or running shoes, or pizza,

you've also got to plan for inflation's longer-term effects on the necessities of life, like shelter, food and health care.

The best solution is making investments that grow in value. That generally doesn't happen when your investments are in accounts that pay little more than the inflation rate. The higher your **real rate of return**, or what you earn after taxes and inflation, the better off you'll be in the long run.

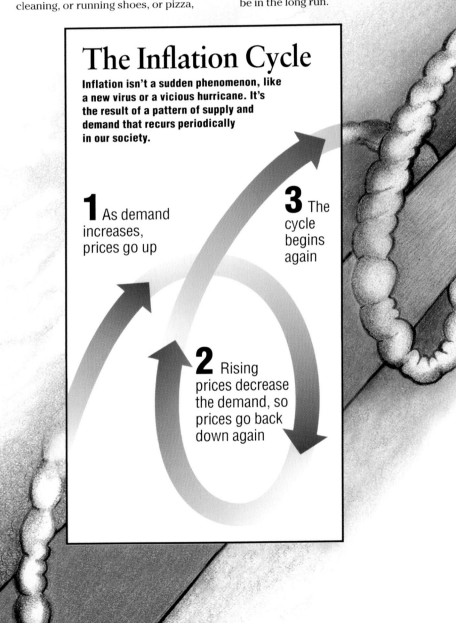

The Inflation Cycle

Inflation isn't a sudden phenomenon, like a new virus or a vicious hurricane. It's the result of a pattern of supply and demand that recurs periodically in our society.

1 As demand increases, prices go up

3 The cycle begins again

2 Rising prices decrease the demand, so prices go back down again

The inflation rate varies from year to year, and since 1926, has averaged

3.1% a year.

That includes the high point, in 1980, when it hit 14%, and several periods when inflation hovered around 1%.

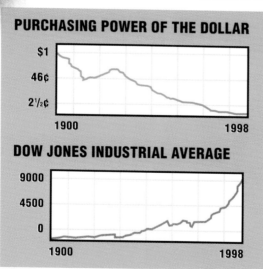

GETTING PERSONAL

It's not that inflation affects you, as a woman, more than it affects a man. But, statistically at least, it will affect you longer because women live, on average, seven years longer than men.

But you can try to fight inflation's effect by investing in stocks and stock mutual funds, which have historically outpaced inflation over the long term. That's the opposite of the way most women have invested in the past, purchasing conservative, fixed-income investments that are the most vulnerable to inflation.

UPS AND DOWNS

As time goes by, the buying power of the dollar declines. That means that if you have the same amount of income each year, your purchasing power gradually shrinks. In contrast, as the chart here suggests, the value of stock and stock mutual fund investments has historically increased as the purchasing power of the dollar has declined.

There have been periods in this century when the dollar actually increased in value and stock prices dipped. But over the long term, the value of stocks has kept rising, and the value of the dollar has kept shrinking.

PURCHASING POWER OF THE DOLLAR

$1
46¢
2½¢

1900   1998

DOW JONES INDUSTRIAL AVERAGE

9000
4500
0

1900   1998

Source: Based on comparisons published by the National Association of Investment Clubs, 1998

MEASURING INFLATION

The Consumer Price Index (CPI) is the most widely used measure of inflation. The index is figured each month by computing the percentage of change for a market basket of 80,000 goods and services. The CPI is measured against the reference period 1982-1984. The CPI determines adjustments in Social Security payments, federal income-tax brackets, and a host of other payments and charges.

Investing, Tax-Wise

Be tax-smart. Do tax-preferred investing first.

Inflation nibbles away at your investment earnings over the years, but taxes can take big bites every year. The solution isn't to avoid investing. Instead, you can include some tax-saving strategies in your overall financial plan.

Many of these strategies involve long-term investments. But there are other ways to keep a bigger share of your earnings. Your tax advisor can explain how to bunch or defer income into a single tax year, for example, or take advantage of tax deductions and credits.

PERSONAL INCOME TAX

TAX ON INTEREST AND DIVIDEND INCOME

SUPPLEMENTAL INCOME AND LOSS

Tax-deferred Investing

You can invest money you've earmarked for your long-term goals through a **tax-deferred** retirement account, and postpone paying taxes on your earnings. The account can be a plan your employer provides, one you set up yourself, or a commercial offering like a deferred annuity or certain kinds of life insurance, as long as it meets IRS requirements.

In some cases, tax-deferred plans have the added advantage of reducing your current income, and therefore your taxes, either because your contribution is excluded from your income, or because you can deduct the amount of your contribution when you figure your taxes (see pages 128–130).

BITING BACK AT TAXES

The Congressional Budget Office calculates that if you earn 8% for 15 years in a tax-deferred retirement plan account, you'll have 37% more after taxes if you're in the 28% tax bracket, and 18% more if you're in the 15% bracket, than you would if you'd been paying taxes all along.

That's why most financial advisors agree that you should participate in any tax-deferred retirement plan that's available at your job, even if it's the only investing you're doing. However, there are some contribution limits on the amount you can put into your tax-deferred accounts each year. And you will pay a penalty in most cases if you withdraw the money before age 59½.

TAX-DEFERRED VS. TAXABLE GROWTH

The chart shows the results of investing a hypothetical $2,000 per year over a 30-year period in taxable and tax-deferred accounts. It assumes the investment earned 8% and that all earnings were reinvested. Taxes are figured for an investor in the 36% federal tax bracket on withdrawal.*

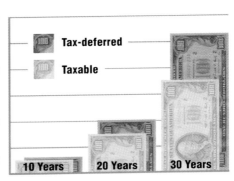

	$300,000		
	$200,000	Tax-deferred	
		Taxable	
	$100,000		
	Investment value	10 Years	20 Years	30 Years

PAPER PROFITS

Another way to avoid paying current taxes is to put your money into growth investments that pay little or nothing now but may be very valuable later.

There are also ways to pass these growth investments along to your heirs without owing tax on the full increase in value. But of course, there is also the risk that you will realize your taxable gains before you die or that your investment will decline rather than grow in value.

A TAXING CONTROVERSY

A long-term **capital gain** is the profit you make on an investment you hold for at least a year. Taxes on capital gains are figured at the long-term capital gains rate, which is always lower than your income tax rate.

TAX ON RETIREMENT INCOME

TAX ON LUMP-SUM DISTRIBUTION

SELF-EMPLOYMENT TAX

SCHEDULE C-BUSINESS INCOME

TAX ON REAL ESTATE INCOME

AND MANY MORE

Tax-exempt Investing

One way to pay less in income taxes is to invest in tax-exempt **municipal bonds**, or **munis**. They're bonds issued by states, or local governments, usually to raise money for building or improvement projects or to pay for day-to-day operating expenses.

Munis usually pay less interest than taxable corporate or Treasury bonds, but you usually don't owe federal tax on your earnings. Your earnings are also exempt from state tax if the bonds are issued in the state where you live.

Tax-exempt investments can make a lot of sense, especially if you're in the higher tax brackets or if you live in a state with high income tax rates, since you'd have to find a taxable investment paying substantially more to equal your tax-exempt earnings.

CAPITAL GAINS AND LOSSES

TAXING EFFECTS

You owe taxes on the dividends and interest you earn on the investments in your regular taxable accounts. Dividends and interest income are taxed at the same rate whether you spend them or reinvest every penny.

TAXABLE EQUIVALENT YIELD

There's an easy formula you can use to figure out how much you'd have to earn on a taxable investment to equal your tax exempt earnings. Suppose, for example, you can earn 5% tax-exempt and you're in the 36% tax bracket. You would need to earn 7.8% on a taxable investment to have the same return.

$$\frac{\text{Tax-exempt yield}}{100 - \text{your tax rate}} = \text{Equivalent taxable yield}$$

for example

$$\frac{5\%}{100 - 36} = .078125$$

Taxable equivalent yield = 7.8%

Financial Advisors

Expert advice is the key to making strong financial decisions.

Would you like to have your investments working harder for you, but you don't know how to go about it? Then ask yourself if you'd be making better decisions if you were getting professional advice. For most people, the answer is yes.

That's because the difference between getting advice and doing without it is often the difference between moving forward toward your goals and being stuck where you are.

Financial advice isn't something you save for emergencies. And it's not an admission of ignorance. Rather, advice works best when it's on going and goal-oriented, helping you to increase your confidence and your investing skills as you develop a financial plan and put it into action.

WHAT FINANCIAL GUIDANCE CAN DO

If you work with a financial advisor, what should you expect to gain?

- Help in defining your goals
- Explanations of investment opportunities and common mistakes
- A structured, individualized strategy for investing
- Advice on specific investments
- Help with evaluating how well your investments are meeting your goals
- A system for recordkeeping
- Help with understanding and managing risk

FINDING THE RIGHT ADVISOR

When you're ready to choose an advisor, you should look for one who'll help you move toward your goals. To make the search easier, it helps if you've thought about the kind of advice you're looking for, and the things you want to accomplish. And remember, the choice is yours: clients pick advisors, not the other way around.

Always ask potential advisors to explain specifically how investments they recommend may accomplish your goals. The more direct the answer, the better you'll feel about following the advice and developing a working relationship with that advisor.

Look for advisors, and financial organizations, that stress your investment concerns. Evaluating financial

ALL IN THE FAMILY

Whether you choose your own advisor or work with one your husband or companion uses is a matter of personal choice, just as your other financial decisions are. Some couples, for example, keep separate accounts and divide household bills. Others pool their money in a joint account. Both ways work.

One advantage of working with a single advisor can be an increased ability to balance your portfolios and simplify tax planning. On the other hand, if you're used to making separate financial decisions, or if you feel that your partner's advisor is not interested in your concerns or answering your questions, finding your own advisor can be the right thing to do.

Your age, the length of your relationship, and other factors can also influence whether it's important to get separate advice. But remember that you're likely to be managing all the investments alone at some point. You don't want to face that responsibility without good financial advice, from an advisor you know.

CHOOSING THE TIME

There's no right time for starting to work with a financial advisor—like your 35th birthday or the day you find the first grey hair. It's one of those situations when it's never too soon—or too late.

But there are occasions that might encourage you to talk to an advisor, either because things are going well, or because they're not:

WHEN TIMES ARE GOOD	WHEN THEY'RE NOT SO GOOD
The balance in your savings account is more than three months' salary	You're afraid of losing your job, or don't expect a salary increase
You just received a big raise	You're facing the likelihood of divorce and you're not sure where you stand financially
You inherited some stocks and bonds, but don't know whether to hold onto them or sell them	You don't have a savings account or a money-market fund
You have several large CDs that are about to mature and the new interest rate is low	You know you'll need money for certain expenses—like education—but don't know how you can manage it

advice was sometimes hard for women in the past, because most investment planning was geared to men. But that's changing, and you can benefit from the increasing emphasis on women as knowledgeable investors and valuable clients.

Be alert to, but not deterred by, advisors who may promote investments that are best for them—not you— because it puts more money into their pockets. If you use the guidelines for choosing an advisor that are suggested in the following pages—with their emphasis on asking good questions and checking references—you should be able to find a qualified advisor interested in building a long-lasting relationship that's centered on your goals.

Sources of Help

If you're looking for professional advice, you can find it.

The good news is that as increasing numbers of investors—including many more women—seek financial advice, they can find it readily. For most people, one of the biggest issues is which type of advisor to work with.

Traditional distinctions between stockbrokers, financial planners and bank investment reps are disappearing, since most professionals now provide advice as part of their services. And, names like planner, consultant and representative increasingly describe people with different areas of expertise.

To help identify those you might want to consult, the chart below describes the range of services various types of advisors can provide.

WHO'S WHO/WHAT'S WHAT

Most financial services institutions (banks, brokerages, mutual funds and insurance companies) provide financial planning and investment advice.

They pay the advisors who work with them either a salary or a commission on the investments they sell. So it's logical that, in many cases, advisors emphasize the advantages of the investments offered by the institutions they work for.

Advisors should be willing to tell you who pays them, and how they earn their income. It's something you should inquire about, because it can help in evaluating the investment choices they offer and in picking what's best for you.

TYPES OF ADVISORS AND ALTERNATE TITLES	INVESTMENT ADVICE OFFERED
BANK INVESTMENT REPRESENTATIVES (Customer Service Representative)	Advise clients on investing through the bank, including annuities, mutual funds, CDs and money funds
CERTIFIED PUBLIC ACCOUNTANTS (CPA)	Provide financial planning and investment advice in certain cases
FINANCIAL PLANNERS (Financial Consultant, Financial Advisor)	Provide financial planning and investment advice; some sell insurance, annuities and securities
INSURANCE AGENTS (Financial Advisor, Financial Planner, Registered Representative)	Provide overall financial planning; some sell certain investments
PRIVATE MONEY MANAGERS (Asset Manager, Personal Banker, Bank Trust Officer)	Oversee assets of affluent clients; this includes making investment decisions
STOCKBROKERS/ FINANCIAL CONSULTANTS (Registered Representative, Account Executive, Financial Advisor)	Provide advice on specific investments, sometimes as part of an overall plan

PROFESSIONAL STANDARDS

Planners are certified or listed by five professional groups:

Certified Financial Planner
(CFP) from Institute of Certified Financial Planners, Denver. Experience and code of ethics required. 10-hour exam. 30 hours continuing education every two years. About 30,000 certified. (800-282-7526)

Chartered Financial Consultant
(ChFC) and Chartered Life Underwriter (CLU), designations granted by the American College, Bryn Mawr PA. Mostly insurance agents certified as financial consultants. (610-526-1000)

IAFP-Listed Planner
The International Association for Financial Planning provides consumer referrals to advisors meeting IAFP standards. 14,000 listed. (800-945-4237)

Fee-Only List of Planners
National Association of Personal Financial Advisors provides listing for comprehensive fee-only planners. 300 listed. (888-FEE ONLY)

Accredited Personal Financial Specialist
(APFS) by American Institute of Certified Public Accountants. Highly selective. Accredits CPAs as financial planners. Involves 8-hour exam. About 1,500 accredited. (800-862-4272)

OTHER SERVICES THEY OFFER	WHERE THEY WORK	HOW THEY GET PAID
Provide day-to-day banking assistance, like reinvestments, loans, transfers, check orders	In most banks and bank branches, increasingly by phone and computer	Salary, and sometimes commissions on sales of annuities and mutual funds
Offer tax planning and preparation. Some sell securities	Private practices, ranging from sole practitioners to international companies	Fees for service
Offer on going evaluation of strategy. Referrals to other experts	Individually or in local or nationwide planning companies	Some commission only, some fee only, or a combination of the two
Sell insurance products including varieties of life insurance and annuities	Individually and at a wide range of companies; also in banks	Primarily on commission
Handle other financial business, including arranging loans, mortgages	At banks and other financial institutions that offer banking services	Usually by fee, sometimes based on size of an overall portfolio they manage
Buy and sell stocks, bonds and mutual funds	At brokerage firms, which can be either local or a branch of a national firm	Commission, often based on the number or volume of trades

Set Your Standards

There are some easy steps to follow in hunting for a financial advisor.

Once you've decided to get financial advice, it's time to look for the right person for the job. Where you look—and the advisor you choose—will depend on your goals and the kind of relationship you want to develop. But there's no lack of choice.

Some advisors help you define your financial plan and then refer you to other professionals to put the plan into action. Others specialize in buying and selling financial products you select. And still others are involved in every phase of your investment life.

While the selection process may sound like a lot of work, it really isn't. A good way to begin is by making a list of people to consider for the job:

1 Ask your family, friends, colleagues or employer if they would recommend the advisors they are working with.

2 Consult your accountant or attorney. Someone you already have a good working relationship with may be qualified to provide financial advice, or can refer you to people who are.

3 Go to seminars, classes, professional meetings and community events on managing your financial affairs.

4 Contact the branch manager at brokerage firms or banks to ask for recommendations. Be sure you make your requirements clear, so that you're directed to advisors with the qualifications you're looking for.

The Qualifications to Look For

Just as you would with any person you plan to hire, determine the qualifications your advisor must have.

EXPERIENCE

While new advisors deserve a chance to prove themselves, they don't have to learn at your expense. Make up your mind that anyone you're paying for advice has to have experience doing what they're doing.

Five years isn't too much to require. Nor is experience working with people whose professions, incomes or life styles are similar to yours. The newer you are to investing, the more important an experienced advisor can be.

REPUTATION

Any advisor you're considering ought to have a good reputation in the field. Referrals from people you trust are important, especially other professionals. Plus, you can—and should—ask for the names of an advisor's current clients with financial situations similar to your own who are willing to act as references.

References are important because there is no complete listing of qualified advisors. Nor does listing, by itself, provide all the information you want.

AFFILIATION

Since well-qualified advisors may work independently, for a local firm, or as part of a large regional or national organization, you probably won't end up judging an advisor strictly by his or her affiliation.

Experts don't agree on which affiliation provides the strongest resource. Some point out that large companies provide superior training programs, supervision and access to research. Others advocate smaller firms where an advisor may be more likely to offer independent advice. They all agree that a proven track record for the person or the firm is critical.

A CALL'S THE WAY

You can telephone each of the people on your preliminary list, explaining that you're looking for a financial advisor. The tone of the conversation, and the kind of information you're given can help you decide whether to schedule an interview.

QUESTION: What if you get called by salespeople you don't know with offers of financial advice and investment opportunities?

ANSWER: If their offers seem to fit your overall plan, you could ask them to send you more information. The only thing you should never do is transact business on the spot. And no legitimate advisor expects you to.

SEVEN WARNING SIGNS

In looking for financial advice, be wary of any advisor who:

- Guarantees you're going to make lots of money
- Insists that an investment has little or no risk
- Seems to oppose investments in mutual funds, stocks and bonds, or CDs
- Advises you to put all of your money in one type of investment
- Recommends investments you don't recognize, and doesn't try to explain them clearly, or says they're too complicated for you to understand
- Argues with or ignores your instructions
- Is vague about the amount of commission or fees he or she will earn

COMPATIBILITY

You've got to be confident in your advisor's skills and feel comfortable working together. Those are judgments you can usually make accurately based on a face-to-face meeting and conversations with some of the advisor's clients.

Among the things many women find important are building a strong bond with an advisor: being encouraged to ask questions, getting clear explanations about investments and investment costs, being listened to and taken seriously and being treated with respect.

EXPERTISE

Can you imagine buying glasses from your dentist, or letting your travel agent fix your car? The same respect for expertise is important in managing your financial affairs. You should be prepared to consult a CPA, for example, or a retirement planning specialist if you are advised to. And, you'll probably have to pay a broker to buy and sell stocks. Expertise does cost money. But it can make a big difference in carrying out your plan.

REGISTERED ADVISORS

A small number of all financial advisors are registered with the Securities and Exchange Commission (SEC). Registration is required only for those who actually sell investments, not for other advisors.

Registered advisors file Part II of Form ADV, which contains a summary of their background and fees. If your advisor is on the list, you can ask to see his or her form by calling the SEC Public Reference Branch (202-942-8090). Part I of the form will report certain disciplinary actions against the advisor, but not current complaints, if there are any. The National Association of Securities Dealers, Inc. (NASD), in association with each state, also tracks the credentials of registered advisors. You can call 800-289-9999.

CHOOSING A FINANCIAL ADVISOR

Conduct an Interview

Good questions are one of the best ways to get good answers.

An interview can make or break any business relationship—especially one that depends on the interaction of advisor and client. But you have to know what you want to find out *before* the interview starts. And you need a clear sense, afterward, of what was said and promised.

1. Make a List of Questions

Make a list of the questions you want to ask—and be sure you ask them. You don't want to get distracted, or be so nervous you miss the information you'll need to make a decision.

Here are some basic questions you might want to include in each interview:

- **What are your ideas about how someone like me should be investing?**
- **What types of investments do you sell the most?**
- **Who are your typical clients and what kinds of investments do most of them make?**
- **How will you help me plan for my retirement (or other goals)?**
- **How often will you review my plan?**
- **How will you keep me up to date on my investments?**
- **What continuing services will I get and how much can I expect to pay each year?**
- **How are you paid for the service you provide?**
- **How are your fees calculated?**
- **Do you have clients who would agree to be references?**

WOMEN AND ADVISORS

As a woman, you may be wondering about the reception you're going to get from the advisors you interview. The good news is, the dynamic between women and financial advisors has started to change for the better, according to OppenheimerFunds research.

In the past, many women felt they weren't getting quality service—that they were talked down to or ignored when they sought help. And advisors, because they believed women didn't understand investing and were slow to act on advice, made little effort to work with them as clients.

But today, it's increasingly clear that what women want—knowledgeable advisors, clear explanations, time to think through what they're doing and an investment plan—is the norm among investors, not the exception. Since most advisors also see those goals as crucial, women are finding advisors and developing strong working relationships with them.

2. Take Notes

Take notes during the discussion. They'll help you remember what's said—and the very act of taking them may encourage more precise answers.

TEAM EFFORT

Investment groups need financial advisors too. If you're in the process of setting up a group, you should put together an interview committee to meet with prospective candidates and make recommendations to the whole group. You'll want to ask most of the same questions you'd ask if you were looking for investment guidance for yourself. In addition, discuss the advisor's experience in working with groups, especially groups of women. Among the things you might expect of your advisor are seminars on specific topics, as well as investment strategies and specific recommendations for implementing them.

When the client is a group, it's also critical to decide from the start who will give the buy and sell orders, and who will act as liaison to the advisor.

3. Evaluate

Prepare a summary of your impression right after the interview and keep it with your notes. The summary will be especially helpful if you interview advisors over several weeks. Check each advisor's references.

4. Choose

You may find that your decision is obvious, even before you've finished the search. Or you may have to draw up a balance sheet to choose between two candidates. At that point, you may find that the reputation of the advisor's firm tilts the scale in one direction or another.

Here are some questions you might want to ask yourself as part of the decision process:

DID THE PERSON I INTERVIEWED

- Treat me with courtesy and respect?
- Listen carefully to my questions and answer them candidly?

DID THE PERSON FIND OUT ABOUT ME AS AN INVESTOR BY

- Asking what my financial goals are?
- Asking about my income and assets?
- Discussing my tolerance for risk?

A TWO-WAY STREET

Interviews are conversations, not performances. The more you know about your goals and your current financial situation, the better you'll be at discussing what you need. And the more eager a qualified advisor will be to work with you.

THE REFERENCE QUESTION

Checking references should be an essential part of your decision-making process, as it should be whenever you hire someone. But just because you know you should do it doesn't always make it easier to ask for references or follow through by checking them.

When you ask your prospective advisor for names, be sure to specify that you want to talk with other clients like yourself—women with similar financial experience, circumstances, or goals. You can expect the advisor to refer you to people who have agreed to talk, presumably because they are pleased with the advice they're getting. You might get the most useful mix, though, if you ask for a list that includes both recent and long-term clients. You should be aware, however, that advisors are not legally required to provide references for potential clients.

When you call, ask each person specifically how she's better off as a result of working with the advisor. The answer should help give you a sense of the kind of investment advice she has received as well as how it meets her goals.

Build a Partnership

When your search for an advisor ends,
the work of building a partnership begins.

If the energy you've spent in finding the right financial advisor is going to pay off, it's important to get off to a good start.

Above all, that means being candid about about your goals and your assets. The more specific you can be, the better.

AVOID MISUNDERSTANDINGS

From the outset, you should put a high premium on clear communication. The best way to ensure that you and your advisor understand each other is to put things in writing.

After you meet, ask your advisor to send you a letter summarizing your goals, your willingness to take risk and your overall financial situation. If the letter reflects what you've said, you should sign and return it, keeping a copy for your records. If the letter is vague, or leaves things out, let your advisor know and ask for a more detailed revised statement.

While the misunderstanding may be something your advisor got wrong, you might also have second thoughts about your own instructions when you see them in black and white.

WHAT TO DO

✓ **Be serious and stick to your plan**

✓ **Read the financial press and material you're given**

✓ **Be inquisitive and ask questions**

✓ **Take a long-term view and give investments a chance to pay off**

Your part in maintaining a relationship with your advisor means staying actively involved. If you don't stick with the investment program you've set up, or keep an eye on how effectively your plan is working, nothing will happen. And that won't be your advisor's fault.

You should let your advisor know when you anticipate major changes in your goals or circumstances, since they may require changes in your investment plan. Any advisor will tell you that financial planning is much harder—sometimes even impossible—after the fact.

If you want your advisor to buy, sell or trade investments in your portfolio, you have to give clear instructions. No advisor is going to

intuit what you want to happen. In any case, you're the boss. It's also a good idea to keep a file of the letters you exchange, your financial statements and all buy/sell confirmations.

Above all, never hesitate to ask questions and insist on clear explanations. Part of the advisor's job is to evaluate investments in relation to each other. But you might want to know what the advisor's stake is if you make one investment rather than another. Most important, be sure the recommendation makes sense for you.

DO YOUR SHARE

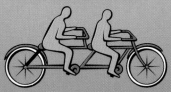

THE ADVISOR'S PERSPECTIVE

Your primary concern, quite legitimately, is whether your advisor will live up to your expectations. But you might find it useful to know how advisors describe a good client. In a recent Oppenheimer-Funds survey, most said they prefer:

- A client who wants to be involved in the decision-making process

- A client who is informed and involved, who has a clear sense of her financial goals and who measures success in terms of how well her investments are meeting those goals

- A client who wants her advisor to generate investment ideas, and provide concrete advice, but who wants to be an equal partner in making the final decisions

TRY AN EXPERIMENT

As you test your new relationship, you might consider starting with a fairly narrow focus. Ask your new advisor to help you invest *for* a specific purpose, like your daughter's education, or *with* a specific amount, like your retirement plan payout. Most advisors will be willing to work on a specific assignment.

Of course, you'll have to assess and act on the advice you're given. But you can also evaluate the way in which the advisor makes investment recommendations and explains them to you. If you're satisfied, you can then make a longer-term arrangement to work together.

WHAT NOT TO DO

✔ **Don't be passive**

✔ **Don't agonize**

✔ **Don't have unreasonable expectations**

✔ **Don't expect to have your hand held**

Although you may work with only one financial advisor, some people are more comfortable using more than one. The point is not so much competition as greater expertise.

For example, you may want to talk to a special advisor about your retirement plans. In most cases, your employer-sponsored investments will be managed separately from your other investments. However, your retirement portfolio can influence the investment decisions you make elsewhere. For example, if your retirement funds are invested in stock of your employer's compa-

CONSIDER TWO ADVISORS

ny, you might decide to avoid buying stocks in the same industry for your personal investment accounts.

You may also work with an accountant or tax attorney, making certain investment decisions to reduce the amount of tax you or your heirs will owe. Accountants, especially those with financial planning expertise, can also provide a valuable second opinion if you have questions about what other advisors are suggesting.

However, if you're working with an advisor to create a long-term investment plan, it doesn't make sense to keep secrets about how much you have invested, or the other advisors you're consulting.

Tailoring a Plan

Work with your advisor in creating a financial plan.

Financial planning is the cornerstone of successful investing. And you can get help developing your plan when you work with a financial advisor.

In looking for a person to work with, you'll discover that some advisors do planning exclusively, and refer you to other experts when you're ready to put your plan into action. Others incorporate planning into the services they provide, like selling investments or doing tax planning.

Those differences might influence the way you pay your advisor, or the place you meet to conduct business. The bottom line is that you can get the help you need from any qualified advisor with whom you are able to work comfortably.

A NEW SPECIALTY

The financial planning profession is actually a fairly new one. It has evolved in response to the growing, clearly recognized need for experts who can help investors make smart financial decisions. And for millions of new investors, planning has ended the fear or procrastination that kept their money in low-paying savings accounts when it could have been growing in investment accounts.

Financial planning is sometimes criticized—unfairly, many agree—for being too loosely defined. Detractors say that there's no licensing or registration requirement for those who work in the field, and no supervising agency.

In fact, there are a number of highly regarded certification programs (see page 53). Planners also develop their skills through extensive in-house training programs run by planning firms, investment companies and brokerages.

A FORMAL PLAN

A professionally prepared financial plan is sometimes a formal document that describes your current financial situation and goals and provides an overview of investing strategies. It also proposes several different types of investments, as well as insurance, tax planning and other financial advice. If a planner suggests a formal plan, ask to see a typical one, so you'll have a clear sense of what you'll be paying for.

Advocates claim that a formal plan will tell you where you stand, focus your investment strategies and help keep you on track.

WHERE TO GO FOR HELP

While sometimes financial planners come looking for you, the more customary approach is for you to make the first move. If you're not sure where to start, here are some ideas:

- Go to seminars offered in your local library, bank branch, or community center. Some organizations and independent advisors specialize in presentations for women

- Most banks, but not all their branches, offer basic planning services. Pick up information in your branch, or ask someone you've worked with there about whom you should talk to

- Look up financial firms in the yellow pages. Those that offer planning advice may advertise it

- Take advantage of information that's available on your job, or through religious, social or civic organizations

A LESS FORMAL PLAN

Advocates of less formal financial plans maintain that you don't need a costly, multipage document to summarize personal information you provided in the first place, or to describe investment opportunities that are regularly discussed in books, newspapers and magazines.

Instead, they suggest you ask your financial advisor to write a follow-up memo, or report, of your initial meeting, outlining your assets, goals and willingness to take risk. That memo can serve as the foundation for building an investment strategy.

TAILOR-MADE PLANS

One of the major advantages of working with a financial advisor to develop an investment plan is having it custom-fitted to your needs and goals. The more experience your advisor has working with women clients, the more precisely he or she can tailor a plan to suit you.

Woman-centered plans are important for several reasons. For one, you have a longer life expectancy. This means you'll have to emphasize growth investments that will enable you to live comfortably for 20, 30 or more years after retirement. Your life insurance needs are also different from many men's, since you're less likely to have to worry about providing security for a surviving spouse.

A PLAN THAT WORKED

In 1944, when Anne Scheiber retired from the IRS, she'd saved $5,000. But when she died in 1995, at age 101, she left an estate worth more than $22 million to Yeshiva University. Scholarships in her name will ensure that many young women can afford the educations they seek.

How did someone whose top annual salary was $4,000 build such an impressive fortune? She had a strategy: invest in stocks you believe will grow in value, reinvest your dividends and be patient. And she worked at it diligently.*

A BUYER'S MARKET

When you're working with a financial advisor, you're the one who decides which plan to adopt and which investments to make. Because you control what happens, you can protect yourself from any potential conflict of interest an advisor might have in recommending one investment over another.

- Ask for an evaluation of the costs of each investment, including what you would pay if you changed your mind or wanted to sell it in the future. The advisor will know the answer, or can find it for you. If it's a mutual fund, you can check the prospectus

- Do some comparison shopping before you make your decision about annuities, insurance policies, bonds and other investments where the cost depends in part on the seller's commission. That will tell you if the price you're being quoted is competitive

- Don't act quickly on recommendations. Most of the investments that you'll be considering change price slowly, so you can take time to think it through, or ask for more information. The only time speed pays for the average investor is in trading stocks, and then you're probably working with a familiar advisor attuned to your wishes

Starting to Invest

Advisors can help with both parts of the investment process: choosing investments and making them.

With your goals defined and your plan in place, you're ready to invest. But that doesn't mean you're on your own unless you want to be. There's a long tradition of investors and advisors working together on investment decisions. The only difference is that now you—and women like you—are part of the picture.

First, you have to decide what to buy. Among the things that will influence your decision are the amount of money you have to invest and the information you have about the various investments you're considering. (In the next chapter, you'll find out about mutual funds, stocks and bonds, the investments at the center of most portfolios.)

You'll probably find that a lot of investing is done by telephone. You can give your advisor a buy order, or sometimes call a mutual fund or brokerage house directly. Or you might invest by mail and, increasingly, by computer.

THE RIGHT STUFF

If you're still having trouble thinking of yourself as an investor, it might help to take another look at the qualities that many financial experts consider crucial to investment success. You may be surprised—and reassured—by how well these characteristics describe you and your approach to money matters:

- Willing to admit what you don't understand
- Ready to ask questions and look for the answers
- Open to professional advice
- Deliberate in making a long-term plan and sticking to it
- Disciplined enough to invest regularly and reinvest your earnings
- More concerned with meeting your goals than making a killing

ON-LINE TRADING

Electronic trading, which means buying and selling on-line, is an increasingly popular way to invest. You can open a new account with an on-line brokerage firm, mutual fund company, or other financial institution. Or, if the institution which you're currently using offers on-line trading, you can expand your existing account. On-line trading benefits may include:

- Lower sales charges
- Regularly updated account information
- Immediate access to market prices, research, and relevant news stories

- Price alerts on investments you own
- Opportunity to place buy and sell orders 24 hours a day
- Ability to create model portfolios

COORDINATING YOUR EFFORTS

One advantage of working closely with your financial advisor in making investment decisions is that you'll have help in coordinating your various accounts. These might include your retirement and regular portfolios, or the investments you and your husband or partner are making.

Your advisor can also help you avoid one pitfall that many beginning investors face, by insuring that your holdings aren't concentrated too heavily in just a few investments. As one example, your advisor might suggest ways to balance your long-term investments in growth mutual funds with other investments better suited to achieving your more immediate goals.

WRAPPED PACKAGES

If you're working with an advisor who is affiliated with a bank or a brokerage firm, you may be able to take advantage of a package of services that the institution offers to encourage you to do more of your business with them.

Banks often reduce the amount you pay for checking and borrowing if your combined accounts and investments hit a specific level. Typical incentives include no-fee credit cards, free ATM transactions and lower loan rates. Brokerages also offer a package of banking services, including checking accounts, credit cards and access to loans. They're sometimes referred to as **asset management accounts** and generally include an annual fee.

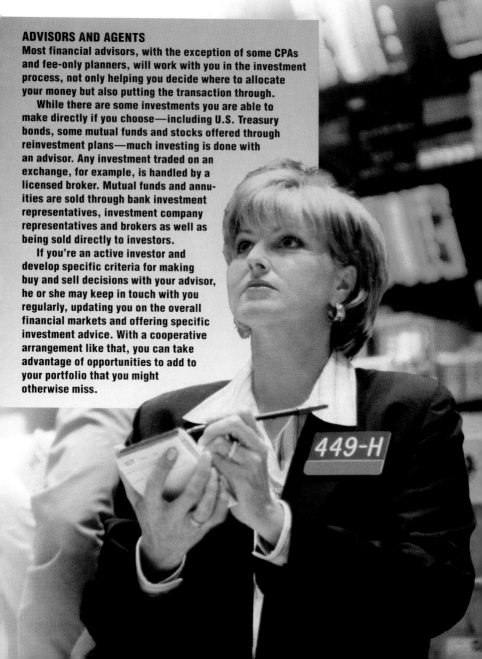

ADVISORS AND AGENTS

Most financial advisors, with the exception of some CPAs and fee-only planners, will work with you in the investment process, not only helping you decide where to allocate your money but also putting the transaction through.

While there are some investments you are able to make directly if you choose—including U.S. Treasury bonds, some mutual funds and stocks offered through reinvestment plans—much investing is done with an advisor. Any investment traded on an exchange, for example, is handled by a licensed broker. Mutual funds and annuities are sold through bank investment representatives, investment company representatives and brokers as well as being sold directly to investors.

If you're an active investor and develop specific criteria for making buy and sell decisions with your advisor, he or she may keep in touch with you regularly, updating you on the overall financial markets and offering specific investment advice. With a cooperative arrangement like that, you can take advantage of opportunities to add to your portfolio that you might otherwise miss.

449-H

The Price of Advice

If you know what investment advice costs, you can make better decisions about what you're spending.

A smart consumer knows what things cost, and is willing to pay the price to get what she wants and needs. That attitude is just as important in investing as it is in selecting food, shelter and clothing.

You can evaluate the advice you're paying for by weighing what it costs against what you gain. If you know, for example, that you'd still be putting off investment planning if you weren't talking regularly to your advisor, you're probably convinced that you're getting your money's worth. Or, if the mutual fund you bought to help pay for your child's education has increased in value, you're confident that the commission you paid was well spent.

Of course, there are times when even the best advice doesn't work, or when investments don't make money. You have to pay for that, too. But over the long haul, most people find that the cost of professional help pays for itself.

FIVE WAYS TO PAY

You pay for financial advice and for the investments you make in one of five ways, depending on the advisor you use and what you buy. Sometimes the cost is built into the price of the investments, sometimes it is added to the cost, and sometimes you pay separately. You should ask for a statement of costs from those advisors who don't provide one automatically.

FEE-ONLY
Fee-only planners charge a fee but don't earn commissions on work they do for you.

FEE-BASED
Fee-based advisors charge a fee and may also earn commissions on some of the products they sell.

THE COST OF COMMISSIONS

The advantage of up-front sales commissions is that you can know right from the start what the price will be.

For example, you pay a commission each time you buy and sell stocks. It's rarely more than 2% of the price for an exchange-traded stock and can be as little as a flat $9.95 for an on-line transaction. The charges are added to the sales price or deducted from the selling price and printed clearly on your confirmation statement.

Commissions on load mutual funds vary from company to company and from fund to fund, and are clearly stated in the fund prospectus. The charges may range up to the NASD limit of 8.5%, though they are typically less. Sometimes you pay both when you buy and sell, but frequently only one time or the other. Typically, the charges are subtracted from the amount you invest to buy or receive when you sell.

Insurance companies also pay salespeople a commission on annuity and life insurance products, though the amount is not deducted from the premium you pay, nor is the percentage typically reported to you. Rather it's recovered from the on-going fees you pay.

FEE, FI, FO

Fees can be either flat charges (based on a rate per hour or an estimate of the amount of time the task will take) or a percentage of the assets you invest.

Flat fees—like the $1,000 to $5,000 you might pay for a financial plan—are one-time expenses. Fees based on the value of your mutual fund or managed brokerage account are usually charged annually, and can end up costing more than a commission. That's why it's important to know how the fee schedule works.

DOING IT YOUR WAY

Can you do your planning on your own, and use a financial advisor only to buy and sell? Certainly. You'll have no trouble finding someone ready to work with you in that capacity. The biggest problem you may have, if you're like other self-directed investors—especially those that are just starting out—is following through on your intentions.

On the other hand, there's lots of excellent information available about financial planning and investing in books, newspapers and journals, from mutual fund companies, on-line over the Internet and in other computer programs. You can use this information to develop your expertise, define your strategy and choose investments.

Your investment costs, if you do the spadework yourself, will come from paying the sales commissions on investments that have them, plus management and other fees when they apply.

COMMISSIONED
An advisor who works on commission earns a percentage of the sale as payment.

SALARIED
Some advisors are paid a salary no matter which investments they sell.

HOURLY RATES
Some advisors charge hourly rates but not fees.

BUYER BEWARE

Some investment advisors who earn high commissions on certain products they sell may not always reveal the amount they stand to gain. In fact, a commission may never be mentioned at all.

Commissions on some life insurance policies, for example, may amount to 100% of the first year's premium. However, those costs are often built into the cost of the policy, so you won't know what they are unless you ask. It's not rude to press your questions about costs. It's the only way to decide whether the cost of an investment is justified by its value to your plan.

Some investments pay high commissions to the people who sell them:

- **Some insurance policies**
- **Some tax-deferred annuities**
- **Unit investment trusts**
- **Pension maximization plans**
- **Limited partnerships**

Resolving Problems

Being prepared for problems
can help you resolve them.

Things can go wrong in any
relationship that involves
money, including the one you
have with a financial advisor.
While recognizing the potential for problems doesn't
mean they will happen, it can
minimize the hassle of dealing
with them if they do occur.

GETTING THINGS STRAIGHT

When you and your advisor
disagree about investment decisions, here are two questions to
resolve before you go any further:

- Have you been misled by the information you've been given, or did you
misunderstand it?

- Did your advisor misinterpret your
wishes, were they ignored, or was there
an honest error?

If it was your fault, you'll know better
next time. But if the problem is with your
advisor, you should act to correct it as
quickly as possible.

IF IT'S BROKE

Mistakes do happen when you give buy
or sell orders. For example, your stock
broker might buy a different stock from
the one you intended. Or the money in a
mutual fund could be incorrectly transferred. If you catch the error and report it
promptly, it may be corrected, or **busted**.

You should call your advisor or broker
as soon as you're aware of any problem,
ask what happened and say you want it
resolved. That may be all you need to do,
especially if it was a misunderstanding.
It's always smart, though, to write a letter
confirming your call and indicating the
resolution that you've agreed to.

If the problem isn't settled promptly,
write to your advisor's boss. Explain
exactly what went wrong—and what you
want to happen. The larger the amount
of money involved and the more serious
the problem, the more likely it is you may
have to seek an outside remedy.

If your complaint isn't handled internally, you can then go to your state's
securities division. If that doesn't resolve
your problem, you may be able to use

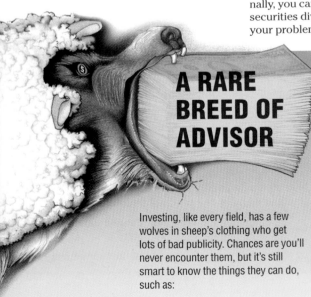

A RARE BREED OF ADVISOR

Investing, like every field, has a few
wolves in sheep's clothing who get
lots of bad publicity. Chances are you'll
never encounter them, but it's still
smart to know the things they can do,
such as:

- Lying about the risks in
particular investments

- Buying and selling without
your permission

- Selling phony or unregis-
tered investments (which
you'll know only when you
try to sell them later on)

- Stealing from your account
(which you'll only know
if you read your monthly
statement carefully)

- Providing false information
about pending law suits or
other legal matters

BINDING ARBITRATION

Arbitration means that you present your complaint, either on your own or with a lawyer's assistance, to a panel of **arbitrators**, or decision makers, put together either by one of the securities exchanges (like NYSE, the New York Stock Exchange), or by the American Arbitration Association.

The arbitrators use the evidence you and your advisor present to make their decision, which is based on their sense of fairness rather than on legal precedent. In most cases the decision is **binding**, which means it can't be appealed. If you're bringing a case, it pays to be prepared with all the supporting documents you can muster. The better your evidence, the stronger your chances of prevailing.

There's a modest fee for arbitration hearings, usually based on the amount of the claim you're making.

TAKING NOTE

Keep track of all the conversations and correspondence with your financial advisor about investment decisions. If your relationship goes sour, you'll have material to bolster your claims. And it's a lot easier and a lot more credible than a record you try to create after the fact.

mediation and finally **binding arbitration**, where a panel of experts will rule on your claim.

If you have an unresolved problem with an insurance agent, you can begin with your state's insurance commission.

If enough money is involved to make it worth your time and expense, you can take a case to court. But before you decide on arbitration or a lawsuit, you should get good legal advice from a specialist in securities law.

PREVENTABLE PROBLEMS

While it doesn't happen often, there have been times when investors have had to deal with problems created by their advisors. You can usually avoid these situations, especially if your advisor knows you're paying careful attention to detail and asking hard questions.

That's why many experts suggest you keep your eyes open for these warning signs:

● An advisor who urges you to make unsuitable investments, like buying more insurance than you need, or putting most of your investments into high risk stocks. Although knowing what's unsuitable means being aware of what each type of investment is designed to do, that shouldn't stop you from questioning your advisor's recommendations. Nor should it deter you from investing

● An advisor who buys and sells too frequently or **churns** your account. It's hard to say what's too frequent, but if you're paying as much or more in commissions as you're making on your investments, that's a sign to act

● An advisor who urges you to buy too much on **margin** by borrowing against your account assets

Making Investments

Stocks, bonds and mutual funds are the substance of a diversified portfolio.

Most investors—from the newest to the most experienced—focus on three types of investments: stocks, bonds and mutual funds. And with good reason. These investments are easy to buy and sell, provide a wide range of choices and have the potential to provide the primary benefit of investing—added financial security.

Each of these investments puts your money to work a little differently, as the descriptions below explain. But it won't take you long to understand how these investments work, or how they may fit into your overall financial plan.

Mutual Funds

A mutual fund invests money that you and others put into the fund. With those resources, a fund can buy many different investments and provide more **diversification**, or variety, than you could achieve on your own for the amount you have to invest. Since each fund is professionally managed, you benefit from that investment expertise. What's more, each fund's prospectus describes the investments it makes, its goals and management style, as well as the level of risk that you're taking.

OTHER INVESTMENT OPPORTUNITIES

CDs
CDs are income investments that pay interest on a specific amount of money for a specific period of time.

REAL ESTATE
Real estate may increase in value and can provide tax advantages.

ANNUITIES
Annuities are tax-deferred investments designed to provide future income, at either a fixed or variable rate.

INVESTMENT VOCABULARY

Stocks and bonds are types of **securities**, a term that once referred to the documents companies and governments issued to represent ownership. Today most investment information, including records of ownership, is stored electronically. You don't get stock or bond certificates—but the name securities has stuck.

It's also helpful to know that investments are sometimes referred to as **products** or **vehicles**, since you're apt to hear those terms. It's one way to suggest the substance of things that you can't actually see or touch.

BUILDING A PORTFOLIO

Your goal as an investor is to build an increasingly larger and more profitable **portfolio**, or collection of investments, most of them probably stocks, bonds and mutual funds. To a lesser degree, you may also put money into cash and cash investments, like money-market funds, CDs and Treasury bills.

You may concentrate on one investment type or another at certain points in your life or under certain market conditions, a process known as **asset allocation** (see pages 102–103). One allocation guideline some women use is to subtract their age from 104. The remainder is the percent of their portfolio they allocate to stocks and stock mutual funds.

You can also include other types of investments in your portfolio to achieve added diversity once you've got the foundation built. One approach is to allocate a small percentage of your investment dollars to more speculative opportunities that might produce major gains but at the same time expose you to the risk of comparable losses.

Stocks

Stocks are **equity** investments, or ownership shares in a business. When you and other investors buy shares, you actually buy part of the business. If it prospers, you make money either because you're paid a share of the profits or because the value of the stock increases, or both. You can own stocks for as long as you like, or buy and sell them regularly, depending on your investment plan. While you can't predict the future, stocks have historically been stronger performers than other types of investments.

Bonds

Bonds are IOUs which corporations and governments issue to you and other investors when you loan them money. They promise to pay back the full amount of the loan at a specific time, plus **interest**, or a percentage of the loan amount, for the use of your money. Investors buy bonds, also known as **fixed-income investments**, because they feel secure knowing that they will get their investment amount back, and because they like the idea of regular interest income.

ART AND COLLECTIBLES

Art and collectibles are speculative investments whose value varies based on quality, availability and fashion.

GOLD

Gold and other precious metals are investments of enduring worth, though their prices vary as supply and demand changes.

FUTURES AND OPTIONS

Futures and options are speculative investments, which change in value as the investments they're derived from change in price.

RISK AND REWARD

With all of these investments there's an expectation of reward and an element of risk. And in general, the greater the chance for a substantial reward, the greater the risk of a loss. Though it's almost impossible to predict any investment's behavior accurately, it's fair to say that you can achieve a better balance between risk and reward with stocks, bonds and mutual funds than with other types of investments.

That doesn't mean you should avoid the rest. In fact, the ideal investment portfolio is often described as a pyramid, with low-risk/low-reward investments providing the base and high-risk/high-reward opportunities at the apex.

Equity and Debt

Every time you make an investment, you buy a piece of the company or get a promise of repayment.

Investing means using money to make money. That happens when:

- You buy an investment that increases in value, pays you **dividends**, or earnings—or does both

- You lend money, giving the borrower the right to use it for a specific period of time, and you collect **interest**, or a percentage of the loan amount as payment

One of your investment goals is **diversification**, or a portfolio with a variety of equity and debt securities. That's because they perform differently and provide different kinds of rewards.

Stocks are equity investments

You own a piece of the company.

ADVANTAGES OF STOCKS

- May increase in value over time, usually faster than the rate of inflation

- May pay dividend income

- Historically provide the best return on investment*

RISKS OF STOCKS

- Volatility, or sharp change in value, especially in the short term

- Performance dependent on company management and overall economy

- Investment in boom periods can mean paying high prices for shares

Bonds are debt investments

You can loan a company money. It pays you back, plus interest.

ADVANTAGES OF BONDS

- Regular income from interest payments

- Return of principal, or investment amount, at end of specified term

- Usually less volatile than equities, so there's less risk of losing principal

RISKS OF BONDS

- Income and principal vulnerable to inflation, or loss of value

- Possibility of losing money if sold before end of investment term

- Investing when interest rates are low means being locked in to less income for term

EQUITY AND DEBT

If you buy certain investments, you have **equity**, or an ownership share. With stocks and mutual funds, for example, you get partial ownership, usually shares in the company or fund that issues them. What you get back as a return on your investment depends on how well the company or fund does and how many shares you own.

If you lend money, as you do when you buy a bond, you've made a **debt** investment. Although those two words seem to contradict each other, it's the most accurate way to describe exchanging your **principal**, or money, for the promise of getting it back, plus interest. Unless the borrower defaults, you can be fairly certain of what you'll earn (the interest) and when you'll get your principal back (the date the loan **matures**, or ends). Knowing how much interest you'll earn, and when you'll receive it, is one of the things that makes bonds appealing.

Mutual funds buy equity and debt investments

You buy shares in a mutual fund, and the fund buys stocks, bonds or other investments. The fund earns interest or dividends on those investments and pays your share of the earnings as dividends.

ADVANTAGES OF STOCK FUNDS

- Generally increase in value over time and often pay dividend income
- Invest in many securities, which reduces investment risk

RISKS OF STOCK FUNDS

- Performance depends on the quality of fund's management
- Even though investment is diversified, there is still market risk

ADVANTAGES OF BOND FUNDS

- Allow more flexibility in price and timing than buying actual bonds
- Provide regular income, which can be reinvested to increase number of shares

RISKS OF BOND FUNDS

- Do not assure return of principal, or pay fixed rate of income
- Earnings vulnerable to inflation and interest rate changes

Stocking up on Stocks

Stocks historically have had the strongest overall performance record in the investment world.

Many people equate investing with buying stocks, and for good reason. Stocks have, over time, produced stronger returns and produced them more consistently than any other investment. Despite that record, some people still hesitate to put money into stocks, perhaps because they're concerned about possible losses.

Most experts agree, though, that buying stocks, either directly or through stock mutual funds, is essential to successful investing. The more you learn about the long-term advantages of owning stocks—despite the risk that stock prices may fluctuate more than other types of investments—the more comfortable you should feel about allocating a larger percentage of your portfolio to them.

What remains is identifying those stocks that are best suited to your overall plan.

PERFORMANCE

The best argument for buying stocks is that historically they have consistently performed better than any other kind of investment. According to Ibbotson Associates, stocks have averaged an 11% return on investment, long-term government bonds, 5.2% and cash, 3.7% over the last 72 years.**

There is, certainly, some risk. Investors have faced a 28% chance of losing money in any single year. But over ten years, the risk dropped to just 2%.

Historical average return for each asset class on a hypothetical $10,000 investment over 20 years.

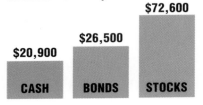

$20,900 — CASH
$26,500 — BONDS
$72,600 — STOCKS

Source: Ibbotson Associates, 1998**

COST

After paying a commission on your initial purchase, stocks don't cost anything to hold on to. True, if you earn dividends or sell at a profit, you owe income tax on what you've made. But there's no tax on **unrealized gains**, or increases in the value of a stock that you still own, and there are no annual fees on the value of your stock portfolio.

The biggest drawback to stocks may be the cost of making the investment, especially for beginning investors. Stock-buying can be expensive because you usually buy **round lots**, or multiples of 100 shares. For example, a stock that sells at $45 a share, will cost you $4,500 plus commission. Buying on **margin**, which means borrowing part of the purchase price from your broker, is an alternative for experienced investors with good-sized portfolios. But it's usually not the way to get started.

SELECTION

The good news is that you have so many choices. You can buy stock in more than 36,000 companies traded in the U.S. alone, which is only one-third of the stocks available around the world. One way that stocks are classified is by size, or **capitalization** (share price times total shares outstanding).

Large companies with long histories, known informally as **blue chips**, are the most stable, the most likely to pay dividends and usually have the highest prices per share. Their market capitalization is usually over $5 billion.

Mid-cap (financial shorthand for mid-sized capitalization) stocks, in middle-sized companies, may have greater growth potential and are generally lower in price than large-company stocks. But they generally provide less income and may pose more risk. Their market capitalization is usually $750 million to $5 billion.

Small companies, or **small-cap** stocks, with a market capitalization of under $750 million, may offer the greatest chance for big price increases and the highest risk of your losing money. There may also be considerably less information available about the performance of small-cap stocks, which makes them harder to evaluate.

BUYING WHAT YOU KNOW

One investment strategy is buying stock in companies whose products and services you know. If what a company provides appeals to you, or fills a need, it's logical to conclude that other people will react in the same way. You can always ask your financial advisor for a professional analysis of a stock's potential, and you can check its recent and long-term performance in the financial press. Or, you can buy stock in the company you work for. In that case, you may be able to save on commissions by buying through an Employee Stock Option Plan, or ESOP.

sometimes managements) change, you can make a large profit if you buy at or near the low point. There have been several examples in recent years where well-known companies have made dramatic recoveries. However, low prices can also be a sign of an ailing company. That's the risk you take.

Trying to decide why certain stock prices are low can be hard, especially if the company doesn't get lots of press coverage. But if value investing appeals to you, it may be worth developing your expertise. The strategy can provide big rewards when you get it right.

CONTRARIAN INVESTING

If you have the nerve, the foresight or just the plain orneriness to buy when the whole market is off and prices in general are lower, you may realize big gains when the market moves higher again. Using the same approach in a more limited way, you can buy on down days, even in booming stock market.

If you're committed to the strategy of concentrating on stocks that other investors are shunning, you're known as a **contrarian**. For this approach to work, however, you have to be willing to hold on even if things get worse before they get better, or if a stock takes a long time to make a comeback.

LOOKING FOR BARGAINS

If you're wondering whether it's possible to get stocks on sale, the answer is yes. While stock discounts don't come on schedule, the way furniture sales do, there are always some stocks that are cheaper than others, including stocks that have fallen in price for one reason or another.

Value stocks are stocks selling at a lower price than the company's reputation or financial situation seems to deserve. One tried-and-true investment strategy is to concentrate on these opportunities, buying inexpensive stocks with the expectation of selling them when the price goes up.

Sometimes, of course, stocks are cheap because a particular company or industry is in trouble. When times (and

Taking Stock

When you know which questions to ask, you'll feel comfortable making stock decisions.

When you're investing in stocks, one of the important things to understand is that what you and other investors buy and sell, and what you're willing to pay, helps determine individual stock prices and the overall performance of the stock market.

If investors are buying a particular stock, the demand increases its price. Similarly, when investors are putting lots of money into stocks, the stock market in general rises. But if they choose other investments instead of stocks, the market in general declines.

One way to invest is to adopt one of the basic stock-buying strategies that has worked well over the years. You can **buy and hold**, or concentrate on building a portfolio of stocks with long-term promise of income, growth, or both.

Or you can **trade**, which means you buy when you expect a stock to increase in value, and sell when it reaches a certain price or increases a certain percentage in value. Though very different, both strategies can provide excellent results.

A TIME TO BUY...

When you're thinking about buying a particular stock, you should ask your financial advisor the answers to several important questions.

- **Are the company's earnings growing? At what rate?**
- **Are the revenues and profits up or down?**
- **How much debt does the company have? Why?**
- **Are its products or services competitive in the markets it reaches?**
- **Are new markets available?**
- **What's going on in the economy at large that might make a difference to the company's success?**
- **What are the strengths and weaknesses of the management team?**

To get the answers, you can check investor updates from the company, read financial news and analyses in papers and magazines and consult with your broker or other financial advisor.

WEIGH THE PRICE

In deciding whether to buy a particular stock, you'll have to determine if it's worth the current price. In essence, you're trying to figure out if it's likely to increase in value so you can sell at a profit, or whether the stock will pay enough in dividends to justify the cost.

Although nobody can accurately predict changes in price, your financial advisor can tell you what experts expect, based on the information currently available. And if you're interested, you can learn to detect recurrent patterns. When interest rates are low, and the amount you can earn with other kinds of investments is limited, for example, the price you pay for stocks may be higher than in periods when you can earn high interest rates on bonds.

SET DOLLAR LIMITS

One approach to stock buying is to set dollar limits for your investments and simply not consider stocks that cost more than your self-imposed ceiling. This strategy lets you create a more diversified portfolio for the same investment amount. Here are some ways, for example, to make a $20,000 investment:

200 shares at $100 per share	=	200 at $45 + 200 at $25 + 200 at $15 + 100 at $30

STOCK EXCHANGE

	52 Weeks Hi	Lo	Stock	Sym	Div	Yld %	PE	Vol 100s
	37 7/8	24 1/8	Reebok	RBK	.30	1.1	13	4326
	34 3/4	24 3/4	ReedInt	RUK	.89e	2.6	...	32
	13 7/8	9 1/4	RegencyHlth	RHS		...	41	143
	18 3/8	15 3/4	RegencyRlty	REG	1.62	9.6	23	37
	41 1/8	24 3/4	ReinsurGp	RGA	.28	.8	14	11
	9 1/4	5 1/4	RelianceGp	REL	.32	4.1	10	1619
	24 5/8	11 7/8 ♣	RelianceStl	RS	.12a	.5	11	138
	51 5/8	33 3/4	ReliaStar	RLR	1.00	2.1	11	1479
	26 5/8	25 1/4	ReliaStar pf		2.50	9.9	...	9
s	27 5/8	17 21/64	Renaissance	RRR		...	16	
n	25 7/8	17	RenHotGrp	RHG		...		
s	27 5/8	10 3/8	RenalTreatm	RXT				
	39 1/8	28 5/8	Repsol	REP				
	15 1/8	9 3/8 ♣	RepG...					
	65	46 7/8	R...					

THE P/E RATIO

One standard measure of a stock's worth is its **price/earnings ratio**, or **p/e**. It's figured by dividing the current price per share by the company's earnings per share for the last four quarters. In this example, for instance, the p/e range of the stocks shown is from 10 to 41.

A p/e goes up when investors are willing to pay increasingly higher prices for a stock because they believe they'll make money. And while no ratio is too low or too high, some analysts question whether investors can make money on stocks with very high p/e's. The same kind of questions surround an exceptionally low p/e, which can indicate a good buy—or a company that investors think is in trouble.

AND A TIME TO SELL

Buying the right stocks will have a major impact on how well your investment portfolio does. But don't underestimate the importance of selling at the right time. In fact, it's just as important to have a strategy for selling as it is for buying. Here's a list of some guidelines that investors follow. Obviously, you can't adopt them all since some contradict others, but you can use them selectively in developing your style of investing:

- **Sell any investment that drops a predetermined percent in value, to limit your losses**
- **Sell any investment that gains a predetermined percent in value; holding out for a 100% gain can rob you of an excellent profit**
- **Sell investments that are down at the end of your tax year if you can use the loss to offset capital gains on your income tax**
- **Sell if there's a major change in the company's stability or direction**

LOOK AT BENCHMARKS

One way to gauge how well your stock portfolio is doing is to look at it in relation to the way the stock market in general is performing. The best-known measure is the **Dow Jones Industrial Average (DJIA)**, whose ups and downs are always in the news. Since the DJIA monitors 30 major industrial companies, though, it may not reflect your personal portfolio. More extensive benchmarks are readily available in the financial pages of your newspaper, in other financial publications and on-line by computer.

If most of your stock is in large companies, the **Standard & Poor's 500-stock Index (S&P 500)** is the one to watch. It tracks the performance of a broad base of widely held stocks in different sectors of the economy. And if you have investments in a wider range of stocks, you can look at the **Wilshire 5000**, which tracks the stocks traded on the NYSE, AMEX and Nasdaq Stock Market. If your portfolio consistently performs more poorly than the index you're using as a benchmark, it's probably time to reevaluate your holdings.

You can also judge the performance of an individual stock by comparing it to an industry-specific index, which companies include in their annual proxy statements. If you discover, for example, that most utility company stocks are prospering while the one you own is not, you may decide to sell and invest your money elsewhere.

The monthly statement you get from a broker or financial advisor doesn't include index information, but it does give you information that you can use to track performance, including current stock prices and your annual dividend earnings. More comprehensive statements also show the original price you paid, and your unrealized gains and losses.

Bonds: The Basics

Companies and governments pay for some of their expenses by borrowing money from individual investors.

Just as you might borrow money for major expenses if you don't have enough in the bank, so do businesses and governments. Sometimes they borrow from a bank, as you would to get a mortgage for a new home. But they can also borrow by **issuing** a bond that promises to pay investors a fixed percentage of interest for the use of their money.

When you buy a bond, you're really lending money for a certain period of time

The bond issuer promises to pay you back, plus interest

THE VALUE OF DEBT

From an investor's standpoint, what bonds provide is a steady stream of interest income. In retirement, for example, your bond interest may be an essential source of income. In fact, that's one reason many financial advisors suggest increasing the amount you have invested in bonds as you get older.

Even if you don't need the income to live on, interest on bonds can provide a regular infusion of cash for your investment account. For example, suppose you had $25,000 in bonds earning 8% interest that paid you $2,000 a year, probably in two $1,000 payments. That money could provide a healthy boost to a mutual fund account or pay for 200 shares of a $10 growth stock.*

The only thing that doesn't make sense while you're building your portfolio is putting the interest you're earning in your checking account and paying day-to-day bills with it.

INFLATION BITES

The chief limitation of bonds, from the perspective of long-term financial security, is that both **principal**, or the amount you invest, and interest are vulnerable to inflation.

If a $1,000 bond pays 6% interest each year for ten years, the $60 will buy less the tenth year than it did the first. If that's the money you're using to buy athletic shoes, for instance, you might find yourself short at the checkout counter.

The same is true with your principal. The amount you get back when the bond matures has less purchasing power than the same amount when you invested it. The one thing that will probably cost the same is another bond.

WHAT BONDS COST

Investing in bonds can help you diversify your portfolio and provide a steady source of income. A bond's initial selling price—usually $1,000—is also known as its **par value**. That's the amount you get back when the bond matures, and it's the base on which the interest payments are figured. However, some bonds may require an investment of $10,000 or more. The price tag can make bonds hard to afford, especially if you're just starting to build an investment portfolio.

It can also be hard to diversify your bond investments, since each purchase requires a substantial sum. But there are strategies you can use to build your bond holdings, by channeling earnings on other investments into bonds, or by using one-time windfalls like an inheritance to get you started. Once you have a foot-hold, you can use the principal you get back when a bond matures to buy another bond.

BONDS AND BOND FUNDS

Many financial advisors suggest buying **bond funds** rather than individual bonds. One reason is that you usually need less money to invest in a fund than you do to make a bond purchase. And since funds own many bonds, you get more diversification in your portfolio.

You, as an investor, don't actually own the bonds, but shares in the bond fund. The fund pays you dividends, or your share of the fund's earnings, based on the interest it receives on its bond holdings.

The fund makes no promise that you'll get your investment back at a particular point in time, the way a bond does. Nor is there a fixed rate of interest, because the fund buys and sells bonds regularly, rather than holding them to maturity. As a result, the fund doesn't earn interest at a single, set rate, but collects from many bonds paying at different rates.

TYPES OF BONDS

While all bonds raise money in essentially the same way, different types of bonds have different characteristics:

CORPORATE BONDS

These bonds are sold by profit-seeking companies as a way of raising money for a range of activities, from expanding operations to building new facilities. Many companies prefer borrowing to issuing additional shares of stock, which dilutes the value of the stock already in the market. The interest you earn is taxable, but corporate bonds generally pay higher interest than other types.

U.S. TREASURY BONDS

Bills, notes and bonds are sold by the government to raise money to finance running the government. Since the government doesn't sell stocks (because there is nothing to own), the only way it can raise money is by collecting taxes and issuing bonds. You owe federal income taxes on the interest you earn, but not state or local taxes.

MUNICIPAL BONDS

Sold by state and local governments, these bonds raise money to pay for a wide array of projects and expenses, and sometimes the actual operation of the government. You owe no federal tax on municipal bonds, and generally no state or local tax on bonds issued by the municipality where you live.

For example, if you live in New York and buy New York State bonds, you owe no tax on the interest you earn. But if you live in California and buy New York bonds, you will owe tax on your earnings to California.

AGENCY BONDS

These bonds are issued by various government agencies, both in Washington and around the country. Among the best known are those that provide mortgage money (especially GNMAs, widely known as Ginnie Maes). The interest is taxable, so the rates are generally slightly higher than on other government bonds.

Bond Issues

Whatever your investment goals, there's a role for bonds in your portfolio.

If you buy and hold bonds for the interest they pay, they are an easy investment to manage. They don't require constant attention, they don't cost anything to maintain, and in the era of electronic record-keeping they can't even get lost. Over time they will provide a dependable source of investment income. Some years, in fact, bonds perform better than stocks.

But if you find passive investing too dull, you can approach bonds differently. Increasingly, investors trade bonds to take advantage of shifting interest rates. Or you can put money into riskier offerings—known as high-yield, or **junk bonds**—the same way you would invest in more speculative stocks.

BUYING TO HOLD

When you buy bonds and hold them until they mature, you know from the start how much you'll earn in interest and when the principal will be repaid.

Only two things can interfere with your expectations: if the issuer **defaults**, or fails to pay the interest or return the principal, or if the bond is **called**, which means the issuer redeems the bond early by paying back the principal. That happens, most often, if the interest rate you're earning is higher than current rates, and the issuer can save money by paying you off and issuing new, lower-paying bonds.

If you're considering a buy-and-hold approach to bonds, here are some suggestions experts make:

- **Investigate a bond's rating before you buy, to evaluate the balance between risk and reward**
- **Check a bond's earliest call date, to determine how long the income is assured**
- **Consider tax-exempt municipal bonds, including tax-exempt zero-coupon bonds, to keep more of your earnings**

MAKING THE INVESTMENT

You can buy bonds through stockbrokers and banks, or in the case of U.S. Treasurys, directly through the Federal Reserve bank. If you buy when the bonds are issued, there's usually no commission since the borrower pays the expense of bringing the bond to market. To buy new issues you usually need to work with a brokerage company that **underwrites**, or sells, the bonds and a financial advisor who knows that you're interested.

If you buy existing bonds, you pay a commission or a **markup**, though not more than 5%. Brokers should tell you the sales cost, if you ask. But unlike stock transactions, where the broker's commission is shown on the confirmation statement as a separate item, the cost of buying bonds isn't stated directly and can be more than you think.

Transaction markups are generally not disclosed, and the bond price you're quoted by one broker may be different from the price for the same bond quoted by another. That means comparison shopping not only pays—it's a necessity.

You can often get a good price if you buy bonds a broker **makes a market in**, which means has a supply of on hand. Or you can buy through a broker who will negotiate the purchase price **over the counter**—which today actually means on the phone.

USING TREASURY DIRECT

If you want to buy federal bills, notes and bonds using a Treasury Direct account and save on all the brokerage fees and other transaction costs, you can get the forms you need to set one up from your local bank or from the Federal Reserve Bank in your area.

You send a check to invest, and the interest and principal are paid directly into your bank account. The major drawback: if you sell before the maturity date, you have to transfer your bond to a broker and pay a commission on the sale.

THE TERM'S THE THING

When you buy bonds, one decision you have to make is how long you want to tie up your money. Unlike stocks or most mutual funds, bonds **mature**, or end, at a specific time.

One advantage is that you can time bonds to mature when you need the money—to pay your child's tuition bills, for example. And by staggering the maturity dates, you can usually make sure that you'll have cash on hand when you need it.

In general, issuers offer a higher rate of interest on **long-term** bonds to offset the risk of tying up your money. The approximate **spread**, or difference between 13-week Treasury bills and 30-year Treasury bonds, for example, was 2.15% in April 1996, 4.85% for bills vs. 7% for bonds.

The advantage of **short-term** Treasury bills is that they are excellent places to park your cash while you're waiting to make an investment. They're safe, they pay more than savings accounts, and they mature in 13, 26 or 52 weeks. Or, you can choose the middle ground, bonds with terms between two and ten years. The interest is usually higher on **intermediate** than on **short-term bonds**, and they can fit well into an overall financial plan.

BUYING AND SELLING

While you may not have considered **trading**, or buying and selling, bonds, you may find it's one way to keep your investment strategy on target. For example, if you want to keep a certain percentage of your assets in bonds and one of your bonds is called, you'll have the principal to invest. If interest rates on new bonds are low, you might prefer to buy an older, higher-paying one in the **secondary market**, where bonds that have already been issued are traded. Or, if you own a high-interest bond when the rate on newly issued bonds is low, you could sell it for more than you paid and use the money to make a different kind of investment.

Before you trade, though, experts suggest that you:

- **Check prices with different brokers to be sure you're getting the best deal**
- **Evaluate previously issued bonds as carefully as you would newly issued ones**
- **Avoid bonds that change dramatically in price, to prevent big losses if you do have to sell**

NEW YORK BONDS

Bonds	Cur Yld	Vol	Close	Net Chg.
AMR 9s16	8.3	15	108	+ ½
AMR 6⅞24	CV	3	114¾	− ½
ATT 4¾98	4.9	25	97¼	...
ATT 6s00	6.0	25	99¼	...
ATT 5⅛01	5.4	17	94¼	+ ¼
ATT 7⅞02	6.9	37	103⅛	+ ¾
ATT 6¾04	6.7	89	101	+ ¼
ATT 7½06	7.1	31	105¼	
ATT	7.2	5		

| LglsLt 8 |
| LglsLt 9 |
| LglsLt |
| LglsL |
| LglsL |
| Lgls |
| MC |

PRICE AND RATE

If you buy or sell bonds already in the market, you'll find their price, listed here under **close**, is more or less than the par value of $1,000. That's because a bond's price in the secondary market is determined by the interest it is paying and its term.

If the interest is higher than what's being offered on newly issued bonds, the price of the old bond will be more than par, since it will be attractive to investors. If the interest is less than the rate the new bonds are paying, the old bond is less attractive and will trade at less than its par value. In this example, the AMR bond paying 9% is selling above par, at 108, or $1,080. The ATT bond paying 5⅛, or 5.125%, is selling below par at 94¼, or $942.50. If you pay more, it's known as **buying at premium**, and if you pay less, it's known as **buying at discount**.*

FROM COUPON TO ZERO COUPON

Once upon a time, you collected your bond interest by clipping a **coupon**, or piece of paper, attached to your bond certificate and taking it to the bank. Today, in the age of electronic record keeping, you don't have to bother with coupons. Payments are mailed.

You can also buy **zero-coupon bonds**. You collect no interest during the term of the bond. Instead, the interest accumulates, so that the amount you collect at maturity is more than the amount you invested. But the value of zero-coupon bonds is unpredictable in the secondary market.

Mutual Funds: Investing Together

Mutual funds rely on investor money and management expertise.

INVESTORS buy shares in a mutual fund

and receive distributions from the fund's profits

When you invest in a mutual fund, you're part of a team that includes investors and an investment company, which can be a mutual fund company, bank or brokerage firm. You and other investors buy shares in a fund the investment company offers, and your collective assets are invested by a professional manager who decides what and when to buy and sell.

This management expertise is one of the main advantages of investing in a mutual fund as opposed to buying stocks and bonds on your own.

Another reason for investors' enthusiasm for mutual funds is that there's something for everyone. Whatever your financial goals, you can find a mutual fund—or a portfolio of mutual funds—to help you meet them, no matter how large or small your investment.

BUYING IN, BUILDING UP

Typically you open an account with a mutual fund company by investing in a specific fund. Each company sets its own account minimum, with most falling in the $1,000 to $2,500 range.

Once your account is opened, you can add to it as frequently or infrequently as you like. All funds set a minimum for additional investments, but sometimes it's as little as $25 and rarely more than $100.

Even if you're adding only small amounts each time you invest, you can build a sizable nest egg over the years. And, there's nothing to prevent you from putting in substantially more than the minimum whenever you can.

WHAT YOU GET

Each time you invest, you buy more shares. In effect, you're buying the right to make money when the fund does well. That happens when it earns interest or dividends from its investments, sells them at a profit, or both. The fund pays you and other shareholders the earnings as dividends, and the profit from sales as capital gains. Together, they're known as **distributions**.

You can use the distributions from the fund as a source of income, or you can **reinvest** them. That means you funnel them back into your account to buy additional shares. The advantage of reinvesting, of course, is that you steadily increase the number of shares you own, even if you aren't adding new money to

OPEN-ENDED OPPORTUNITY

In most cases, the sky's the limit on the amount you can invest in a mutual fund. That's because most of the 9,000 funds on the market today are **open-ended funds**. As investors buy more shares, the funds increase the size of their portfolios by making more investments.

In contrast, **closed-end funds** sell a limited number of shares to interested investors. Existing shares are bought and sold on the stock exchanges, like shares of stock. In fact, closed-end funds are sometimes called **exchange-traded funds**.

Sometimes, though, if an open-ended fund is wildly successful, and the mutual fund company is concerned that it could lose some of its trading flexibility, the company may close the fund to most new investors—although if you already own shares, you can continue adding to your account.

When that happens, the company may open a second fund with similar objectives—and even the same manager—to capitalize on investor interest.

THE GROWING FUND MARKET

The first mutual fund in the U.S. opened for business in 1924. By 1940, there were fewer than 80 funds, and by 1960 only 161—all of them stock funds. By 1980, there were 564, almost a quarter of them bond funds. In 1998, the number was 9,000 funds and still growing.

MUTUAL FUND COMPANY

Successful investments add value to the fund

FUND MANAGER

The fund manager buys stocks, bonds or other investments for their income and/or growth potential

the fund. And most funds make it easy, and cheap, to reinvest. All you have to do is choose the reinvestment option when you open your account. The fund takes care of the details—usually without charging a fee.

HOW MUTUAL FUNDS WORK

A mutual fund combines your money with the money of other investors, and uses those assets to build its portfolio. The manager focuses on investments that match the fund's objectives in order to produce the kind of results you were seeking when you selected the fund.

But since you and other investors can **redeem** your shares, or sell them back to the fund at any time, the manager must also keep the fund liquid enough to pay you the current value of any shares you redeem. That means keeping some assets available in cash and holding others that can be traded quickly, hopefully at a profit.

Funds vary by styles and objectives. For example, some managers emphasize value, which means seeking low prices. Others concentrate on earning dependable dividends. And some trade more frequently than others, and so have a higher **turnover rate**. Because style can affect performance, it's something savvy investors consider when choosing a fund.

UNCLE SAM'S SHARE OF THE PROFIT

Whether you decide to take your distributions or reinvest them, you'll owe income tax on the total amount, with the following exceptions:

- If you invest in **municipal bond funds**, also known as tax-free funds, your dividends aren't usually taxed, but your capital gains are. The fund sends a Form 1099 at the end of the year telling you what's taxable

- If your mutual fund holdings are part of your IRA or other qualified retirement plan, all the distributions are tax-deferred, and you owe no tax on them until you begin to redeem, or take money out of your fund

Mutual Fund Marketplace

Whether you like them plain or fancy, you can find funds to match your taste.

The point of investing in mutual funds—like the point of investing in anything—is meeting your financial goals. One major appeal of the mutual fund market is that you can almost always find a fund that appeals to you.

Before you decide which funds to buy, however, it helps to know about the kinds of funds there are, and their basic investment objectives. Otherwise, you could end up buying a popular fund that's actually too risky—or too conservative for your investment plan. Each fund's investment objective, its level of risk and investment strategy, are explained in the **prospectus** the fund company sends before you invest.

A SHOPPER'S GUIDE

In narrowing your selection, you might choose from a cross section of funds with different objectives.

MUNICIPAL BOND FUNDS

buy tax-exempt bonds. Some funds concentrate on bonds issued by a single state, while others buy bonds from many states. You generally don't owe federal taxes on the dividends from these funds, but you may owe state taxes.

GNMA FUNDS buy bonds backed by a pool of government-insured mortgages. They provide income and return of principal, though what you earn is influenced by changes in the interest rate. Since GNMA bonds themselves come in large denominations, funds make them accessible to individual investors.

GROWTH FUNDS are stock funds that invest in growing companies expected to increase in value, thereby increasing the value of the fund that owns shares in them. Some funds concentrate on companies of the same size—large-, mid- or small-cap and others buy all three sizes. Growth funds are usually most valuable as long-term investments.

AGGRESSIVE GROWTH FUNDS

take bigger risks than other growth funds, by investing in start-up companies or those that are currently in financial trouble. Even though some investments will fail, the fund expects that others will succeed. These funds, also known as **emerging growth funds**, are best suited for long-term investment.

VALUE FUNDS are stock funds that invest in **undervalued companies**—those whose prices are lower than they seem to be worth, or have dropped in value, or are currently out of favor. The fund expects that prices of its holdings will increase as more investors buy the stock, or the companies turn themselves around and resolve the problems that have kept investors away.

THE FIRST CUT

All mutual funds are grouped into three broad categories: stock funds, bond funds and money-market funds. Each type has further subdivisions, to suit different investor goals.

Stock funds buy shares of publicly traded corporations—the same ones you can buy as an individual. But they buy more shares and build more diversified portfolios than you could on your own. You can choose funds designed to provide growth, income or a combination of the two, and reinvest your earnings.

Bond funds buy bonds issued by corporations, federal governments (including the U.S. Treasury), municipal (state and local) governments and government agencies. Bond funds produce income, but your earnings can be reinvested to buy additional fund shares, so your investment can also grow.

Money-market funds invest in short-term corporate and government bonds and other debt. They provide current income at about the same rate of interest as CDs, and can be used as checking accounts. Some funds set a minimum amount for each check—often $250 to $500—but let you write an unlimited number.

INCOME FUNDS invest to produce current income. The amount of income generally reflects the riskiness of the investments the fund is making. The greater the risk, the higher the income. While income funds are frequently bond funds, **equity income funds** and **total return funds** are predominately stock funds, and **balanced funds** are part stock and part bond.

HIGH-YIELD FUNDS are bond funds that invest in low-rated or unrated bonds, sometimes called **junk bonds**. Because they may produce high income, they are frequently appealing to investors who are willing to assume the risk that junk bonds might default.

SECTOR FUNDS are stock funds that concentrate all of their trading in a particular area of the economy, such as utilities, transportation, or technology. A sector fund performs significantly better—or worse—than other funds, depending on how the particular sector is doing.

GROWTH AND INCOME FUNDS are stock funds that invest primarily in companies poised for growth and paying high dividends. Since they buy established stocks with strong performance records, they can provide more consistent returns than funds investing more speculatively.

QUANTITATIVE FUNDS (sometimes called quant funds) are basically index funds trying to do better than a particular index by concentrating on its strongest securities.

SOCIALLY RESPONSIBLE FUNDS invest only in companies whose manufacturing and marketing policies meet a specific set of social standards. A typical socially responsible fund might avoid tobacco company stock or companies with poor environmental or equal opportunity records. These funds, which include stock, bond and index funds, aren't tracked as a separate category, but promote themselves as being socially conscious.

Specialized Funds

Whatever breed of mutual fund you're looking for, chances are you'll find it.

Most mutual fund companies sponsor a number of different funds, each with a specific investment goal. Taken together, a company's offerings are referred to as a **family of funds**.

As an investor, you can select several funds from the same family or just a fund or two. One advantage of being part of a family is that you can open an account in an additional fund or transfer money easily between funds over the telephone. But it's the rare family that fields top-rated funds in every category. That's the reason many investors own funds in several different fund families.

You can also choose specialized funds, offered by fund companies to meet specific investment objectives.

INDEX FUNDS

The performance of stock and bond investments is measured by a number of different **indexes**. Each index measures the current average performance—up, down or flat—of a certain investment category against a benchmark, or base, determined by its past performance.

The point of an **index fund** is to produce the same results as the index it tracks. Its strategy is to buy and hold all the stocks or bonds included in that index.

In other words, an index fund aims to do as well—but not better than—a particular part of the market. In contrast, most stock or bond funds strive for better results than the market average, and hire professional managers to pursue that goal by choosing investments that they expect will perform well.

Index funds, especially funds that track Standard & Poor's 500-stock Index, are popular with investors. With an index fund, you don't have to worry about choosing among the various funds that are available, and you generally pay lower fees than you do with other kinds of funds.

Some financial advisors have reservations about focusing on index funds. They suggest that index investors may be ignoring opportunities to take advantage of skilled management decisions and potentially higher returns.

Other advisors believe that index fund investors should diversify by buying funds that track different indexes. Their argument is that a range of funds, including some linked to international indexes, can help to balance downturns in some markets with gains in others.

BALANCED FUNDS

While the majority of funds concentrate on either stocks or bonds, some funds buy both. In the case of **balanced funds**, for example, the fund's objective is to provide a one-stop diversified investment with at least 25% stocks and 25% bonds. The advantage of the mix is that the bond income provides some protection against a drop in the value of stocks. The drawback is that balanced funds usually do not perform as well as straight stock funds when equity markets are strong.

INVESTING AROUND THE WORLD

Most financial advisors agree that it's increasingly important to have money invested in other parts of the world. It makes sense both as a **hedge**, or protection against downturns in the U.S. market, and as a way to take advantage of strong economies in other regions or countries.

Since funds do the research, handle the buying and selling and take care of the taxes—all of which can be a hassle for an individual investor—they're often the easiest way to invest overseas. Many of the large fund companies offer a variety of international and global funds, as well as funds that specialize in particular geographic regions. **International funds** generally don't include U.S. investments in their portfolios, while **global funds** may.

In addition to the open-ended mutual funds, you can buy closed-end **country funds**, which invest in a particular country.

LIFE CYCLE FUNDS

One way to get diversity in a single purchase, especially for investors who are just starting out, or who have a limited investment budget, is to buy a **life cycle fund**. These funds channel your investment into a mix of stock and bond funds, shifting the balance among them to suit your investment objectives.

Life cycle funds generally include three to five risk options, with investing styles ranging from aggressive to conservative. You can choose the category that's best suited to your objectives as well as your tolerance for risk. The longer your time frame, the more aggressive you can generally afford to be.

Asset allocation funds also invest in a broad spectrum of investments, shifting their allocations to take advantage of changes in the markets. While many advisors recommend them, some critics feel that this investment style alters the basic strength of mutual funds—long-term investing—and may result in larger fees, making it harder to achieve the best results.

Buying Mutual Funds

Opening a mutual fund account and investing regularly are as easy as 1, 2, 3.

Investing in mutual funds is easier than you think. You can open an account two different ways: through a financial advisor—a dealer, agent, bank representative or broker—or directly with a fund company.

1. Fill out an application

You need a completed application and enough money to meet the minimum investment requirement.

2. Write a check

If you're dealing directly with the fund company, you complete the application and send a check. If you're using an agent, you can write a check or arrange to have your opening investment sent electronically from your bank or brokerage account.

3. Keep investing

To make an additional investment, you can send a check or have the amount transferred directly from your bank or other account on a regular schedule. If your employer offers direct deposit, you can usually arrange to have a portion of your paycheck directly deposited into a fund as well.

ASKING THE QUESTIONS

When you're choosing a mutual fund investment for your portfolio, there are five basic questions to ask about each fund you're considering:

- **Is the fund's objective suited to my financial goals?**
- **Is the fund's performance strong in comparison with other funds with similar objectives?**
- **How do the annual fees compare with fees for similar funds?**
- **What kind of risk does the fund expose me to?**
- **Can I live with that risk?**

THE COST OF BUYING

Some funds add a sales charge—known as a **load**—to the price per share when you buy. The load, a fixed percentage of the amount you're investing, is used to pay commissions to the person or institution providing you with investment advice and handling your transactions. Each fund company sets its own sales charge, up to the legal limit of 8.5%. Most charge less.

Front-end loads, which mean you pay the sales charge when you make the purchase, are the most common. In other cases, **back-end loads** are imposed when you sell your shares within a certain period of time, often five or six years. Some fund companies let you decide the load arrangement you prefer at the time you invest. They may reduce the sales charges if you invest substantial amounts, or even waive fees on some withdrawals, including regular payouts from retirement plan accounts.

Other funds are **no-loads**, which means you pay no sales charge when you buy or sell shares. But many fund companies, including some no-loads, charge an annual fee, called a 12b-1 fee, of up to 1% of your assets, which is used to pay for commissions and marketing.

The fund's prospectus explains its fees, including whether or not there is a sales charge. Or you can find the information in the mutual fund columns that appear in your newspaper.

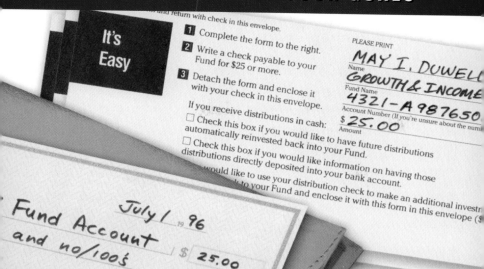

It's Easy

...and return with check in this envelope.

1. Complete the form to the right.
2. Write a check payable to your Fund for $25 or more.
3. Detach the form and enclose it with your check in this envelope.

If you receive distributions in cash:
☐ Check this box if you would like to have future distributions automatically reinvested back into your Fund.
☐ Check this box if you would like information on having those distributions directly deposited into your bank account.
...would like to use your distribution check to make an additional investm... ...to your Fund and enclose it with this form in this envelope ($...

PLEASE PRINT

Name
MAY I. DUWELL
Fund Name
GROWTH & INCOME
Account Number (If you're unsure about the numb...
4321-A 987650
Amount
$25.00

July 1 19 96

Fund Account
and no/100$ $ 25.00
                      DOLLARS

May I. Duwell

DIRECT INVESTMENT PLANS

Direct investing can be an easy and smart way to build your mutual fund account. Usually, funds encourage automatic investment by reducing the minimum for opening an account or making additional purchases. Some mutual fund companies, for example, let you open and add to your account with as little as $25 (rather than the more typical $100 additional investment) if you use their direct investment plans. The lower minimum can make a big difference if you're ready to start investing but don't have a lot of money.

Direct investing also keeps you contributing, cuts down on check writing and helps you budget for investing. Since you can stop participating at any time, there's no real drawback to trying it.

THE ADVICE FACTOR

If you're uncertain about which funds to buy, or tend to put off investment decisions, paying a commission to an advisor who helps you make smart decisions can be money well spent. One question to ask yourself is what funds you would buy on your own. If you don't know, or suspect you wouldn't be investing, an advisor's help can be crucial.

COMPARING TOTAL RETURN

One of the ways to evaluate the mutual funds you're considering is by comparing their **total return**, or the average annual percentage by which each fund has increased in value, including reinvested dividends. You get that information from your financial advisor, from the funds themselves, and in the financial press.

Among the things you'll discover is that over time, load and no-load funds tend to produce similar total returns.

In the short term, paying a load reduces what you get back on your investment. But if you stay invested in a fund, the effect of the sales charge diminishes over time. Information compiled by the research firm Morningstar Inc. shows that after ten years the results for load and no-load funds are essentially equal.

However, if you trade funds frequently, paying repeated sales charges can take a bigger bite of your earnings. But most financial advisors agree that trading isn't the best approach to mutual fund investing in any case.

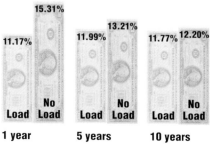

11.17% **No** 15.31%	11.99% **No** 13.21%	11.77% 12.20% **No**
Load Load	Load Load	Load Load
1 year	5 years	10 years

Source: Morningstar, Inc., 1996

Expanding Your Fund Portfolio

As your portfolio grows in value, you can also get the advantage of greater diversity.

Mutual funds are designed for portfolio building, or increasing the number and value of your investments. Because you can reinvest your earnings easily, you can steadily add to the number of shares you own. And the more shares you have, the more reinvestment money they may generate.

Since the typical stock fund owns shares in 100 or more companies, it's usually less vulnerable to declines in value than shares of an individual stock or bonds paying a specific interest rate.

And since there are so many fund varieties—Lipper Analytical Services tracks 21 separate categories—you can get even greater variety and greater opportunity for growth over time by buying funds in a number of different investment categories.

FINDING THE RIGHT FUNDS

Mutual funds are excellent tools for building financial security. But as with all investments, you get the most out of them by choosing the ones that will serve you best. Your financial advisor can help you identify the types of funds well suited to your goals, and work with you to select specific funds to meet your needs.

Before investing, you should always read a fund's prospectus, which you get with the application. It provides basic information, including a statement of the fund's objectives, its fees, an analysis of potential risks and sometimes a report on its performance.

You can compare funds with similar objectives by looking at independent research from firms like Value Line, Morningstar, Inc., and Lipper Analytical Services (available by subscription, in libraries or on-line). You can also expand your reading to include the financial pages of major newspapers, and business and financial magazines.

SIMPLIFIED BUYING

One of the most appealing aspects of mutual fund investing is that when you open or add money to an account, you buy the number of full or fractional shares equal to your investment amount minus sales charge, if any. So if a share costs $20, and you invest $100, you buy five shares.

Slot your investments into a range of funds, diversifying over time

Invest $2,000 every year for 30 years

If you invest $250, you buy 12½ shares. That can be a lot easier than saving until you've accumulated the full price of an investment, the way you usually have to do with stocks and bonds.

To get a sense of how building a mutual fund portfolio works, consider this hypothetical example: You put $166 a month into an equity fund costing $10 a share. Every month you buy 16.6 shares ($166÷10=16.6$), and reinvest your earnings. After a year, assuming the fund provided a 10% return, you'd have approximately 219 shares, or a portfolio worth about $2,191 before taxes.

While that may seem to be modest growth, over 10 years of regular investing, the portfolio could be worth $31,291 before taxes. After 30 years, assuming the same rate of growth, you could have built your fund value to $244,692 before taxes.*

Value of your portfolio after 30 years: $244,692*

PAPER TRIMMING

At the moment, mutual fund companies are working to reduce paperwork by providing consolidated statements that cover your entire portfolio. Sometimes they also include your husband's accounts, yours, and those you hold jointly. But stay tuned: electronic statementing is just around the corner. You'll be able to keep track of your accounts by computer, without opening stacks of mail.

DOLLAR COST AVERAGING

Your mutual funds will grow most effectively if you give them regular cash infusions, either by automatic direct investing, or committing yourself to investing once a month, or more often.

Beside building your nest egg, investing regularly eliminates the worry about choosing the best time to buy. Ideally, of course, a smart investor wants to buy low and sell high. Since in the real world, however, you can't count on doing that, a smart way to avoid paying a high price for your annual investment is to buy in smaller increments on a regular schedule.

Since the share price of every fund moves up and down as the value of its holdings change, buying this way will sometimes cost you more and sometimes less per share. But if you buy high *and* low, your average cost per share may be less than the average share price, as the hypothetical example to the right shows.***

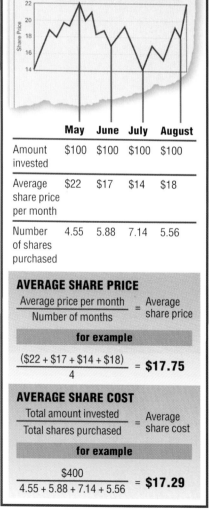

DOLLAR COST AVERAGING

	May	June	July	August
Amount invested	$100	$100	$100	$100
Average share price per month	$22	$17	$14	$18
Number of shares purchased	4.55	5.88	7.14	5.56

AVERAGE SHARE PRICE

$$\frac{\text{Average price per month}}{\text{Number of months}} = \text{Average share price}$$

for example

$$\frac{(\$22 + \$17 + \$14 + \$18)}{4} = \$17.75$$

AVERAGE SHARE COST

$$\frac{\text{Total amount invested}}{\text{Total shares purchased}} = \text{Average share cost}$$

for example

$$\frac{\$400}{4.55 + 5.88 + 7.14 + 5.56} = \$17.29$$

Fund Performance

You win with mutual funds if you're looking for steady progress, not great leaps and bounds.

As convenient as it is to invest in mutual funds, there are things that you, as an investor, should be doing to ensure that your investments are on the right track.

Mutual fund companies make tracking easy, since they compute the value of each fund at the end of every business day. The information is widely available the next morning in the media and on-line using your computer.

That doesn't mean you need to check every day, or even every week. Fund prices and performance change value relatively slowly. But tracking should be a regular part of your investment strategy.

TOTAL RETURN

Total return, or the amount a fund increases in value plus the distributions it pays, is the clearest measure of fund performance. Both the total return and the **percent return**, or total return divided by the cost of the investment, are reported regularly in the press and in updates your fund sends you.

To see how your fund is doing in relation to others with the same objectives, you can compare the percent return you're getting with the average for all of the funds in the same category. Lipper Analytical Services provides those benchmark numbers, which appear regularly in newspaper mutual fund columns.

REINVESTMENT PAYS

According to Ibbotson Associates, if you'd invested $1 in large company stock at year end 1925 it would have been worth $76.07 by year end 1997. But if all the dividends had been reinvested, it would have grown to $1,828.33.** The numbers speak for themselves: reinvestment pays.

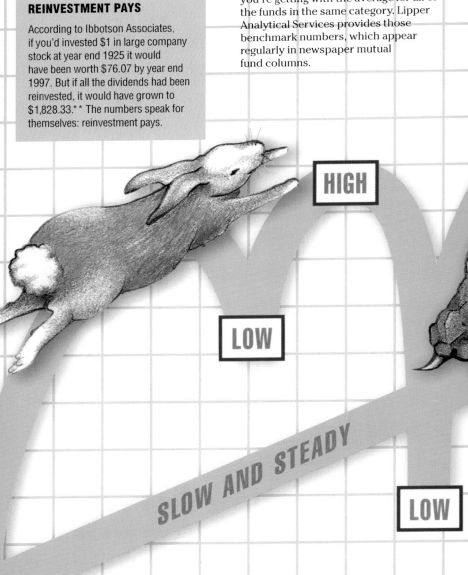

HIGH

LOW

SLOW AND STEADY

LOW

THE IMPACT OF TIME

In judging a fund's performance, it's critical to assess how well it has done, not only in the last year but in the last five years—and in the last ten if the fund has been around that long. The reason? You want to know how well a fund has done in different economic and market climates. While what happened in the past will not predict future results, it's some indication of the fund's ability to perform.

Some funds, for example, do extremely well in **bull markets**, when stocks are booming, but much less well in **bear markets**, when stocks can lose value.

Other funds are better at maintaining a balanced performance—increasing in value when other funds do, but losing less in a downturn. These funds have a lot to recommend them. But there's also evidence that long-term investing can eventually level out the effect of short-term swings in value.

The other thing to remember is that the last extended bear market dates back to 1973–1974, before many of today's top performing funds made their debut. The truth is, there's no accurate way to tell how these funds would perform in a similar downturn in the future.

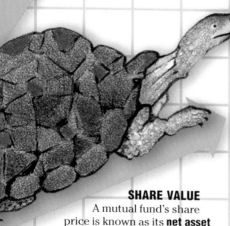

SHARE VALUE

A mutual fund's share price is known as its **net asset value (NAV)**. It's the value of the fund's net assets, divided by the number of outstanding shares. You pay the NAV for each share of a no-load fund, and NAV plus sales charge for a load fund. The load price is known as **MOP**, or **maximum offering price**.

You can use changes in a fund's NAV to track performance. But the NAV isn't as reliable an indicator as total return because funds pay out most earnings to shareholders, keeping their value stable.

FEES

All mutual funds have annual management fees, and some have marketing fees known as 12b-1 fees, as well as transaction fees (loads, redemption and exchange fees). Most financial advisors suggest looking for funds with average or below average costs.

The reason is simple: the more you pay in fees, the more your fund has to earn to provide the return on investment you want. For example, if two stock funds earn the same 15%, but Fund A has expenses of 3.5% while Fund B has expenses of 1.5%, you come out ahead with Fund B.

The good news is that you can easily check the fees before you buy. Both a fee schedule and **expense ratio**—annual operating expenses divided by average net assets—are shown in a fund's prospectus, along with an estimate of the fees you can expect to pay while you own the fund.

TYPICAL EXPENSE RATIOS

The chart below reports the average expense ratio, plus the highs and lows, for different types of funds. Note that some types of funds are more expensive to operate than others, usually because they require more active research and management. International equity funds, for example, tend to have higher fees, while government bond funds tend to cost less. Index funds often cost the least.*

Fund category	Expense ratio		
	Low	Medium	High
Growth	0.25%	1.31%	2.93%
Growth and income	0.20%	1.20%	2.50%
International funds	0.47%	1.65%	3.07%
High current yield	0.28%	1.24%	2.16%
General US Treasury	0.40%	1.11%	2.17%
General bond	0.50%	1.03%	1.85%

Source: Lipper Analytical Services, 1998

LOOKING AHEAD

Most financial experts stress that mutual funds are best suited for long-term investing. They believe you should be less concerned with short-term peaks and valleys, or with the top funds of the year, than with sticking with dependable funds that fit your investment strategy.

Basics of Investing

If you concentrate on the principles, you'll have the elements of an investment strategy.

You can begin to invest with confidence and grow more comfortable with investing by following two basic principles:

- You manage **risk**, or the chance of getting poor returns, by diversifying, or making a variety of investments

- You measure investment reward by **return**, or the money you get back for what you put in

VOLATILITY
is how much and how quickly the value of an investment changes

RISK
is the chance you take of getting a poor return or losing money

DIVERSIFICATION
is making several different types of investments rather than just one or two

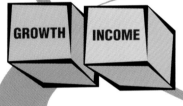

GROWTH INCOME

ALLOCATION
is deciding what percentage of your portfolio goes into stocks, bonds and cash—or mutual funds that invest in them

PLANNING AND MONITORING

An important part of financial planning is anticipating how well investments will perform. That means weighing the risks you're taking against the rewards you can potentially receive. In addition, you need to monitor return and yield so you can judge how well you're actually doing.

Another key to successful investing is having a broad perspective. This means looking at a range of investments in relation to one another rather than zeroing in on one or two. You also have to set your sights on long-term rewards, ignoring the inevitable short-term swings in the market place.

TWO STRATEGIC APPROACHES

You might decide that the way to meet your long-term goals is to put money into equities you expect to grow in value. This strategy helps you concentrate on specific types of investments, first on equities and then more narrowly still on those that seem likely to perform best over the long haul.

If you are investing to meet both long- and short-term goals, you might select stocks and stock mutual funds providing both growth and income in addition to those emphasizing growth alone. By reinvesting your dividends and other gains, it's possible to build your investment base more quickly and still benefit from long-term growth. Or, if you've retired and want to begin collecting income from your portfolio, you may want to shift some of your assets to income-producing investments like bonds.

Any strategy, however, requires attention to basic details: understanding risk, volatility, diversification, asset allocation and how to measure and evaluate yield and return.

RETURN

is what you get back, based on what you invest, usually measured on an annual basis

Total Return

1 Yr		3 Yr-R		5 Yr-R	
+14.5	E	+14.3	C	+15.8	B
+13.1	E	+9.8	E	+13.0	D
+14.5	B	NS	..	NS	..
+13.5	D	+10.6	C	+11.8	C

YIELD

is the income you receive as a percent of what your investment cost you

ONE YEAR CD

ANNUAL PERCENTAGE YIELD
6.25%

INTEREST RATE
6.00%

KEEPING ON TRACK

Picking the right investments is only the first step in achieving your financial goals. You also have to monitor their performance regularly, asking whether these investments are still right for your portfolio as your goals shift and your life style changes. And—this is where many investors falter—you have to be ready to make adjustments, sometimes even major changes, when you redefine your goals, or when the investments you've made aren't performing as well as you expected.

It can be hard to move in new directions. If you feel comfortable relying on the investments you already know—perhaps CDs, money-market accounts, or stock in the company you work for—there's always the temptation to stick with them. And while they may have their place in your investment plan, tying up your money in one or two places exposes you to greater investment risk.

A DISTINCTIVE DIFFERENCE

Saving and investing both have a place in your financial plan, but they're not the same:

Saving is holding money, usually in bank accounts or money-market funds, for a specific *short-term* purpose.

Investing is buying things of value—particularly mutual funds, stocks and bonds—that provide income or increase in worth over the *long term*.

Though your savings earn interest, they may actually shrink in value over time. That's because the interest you earn is rarely more than the rate of inflation. For example, if you put $10,000 in a savings account earning 4% interest, you'd accumulate $20,300 after 18 years. If inflation averaged 4% per year, your savings would actually be worth $10,150. After taxes, you'd have less buying power than when you started.

But if you'd invested the money, earning 8% for 18 years, you'd have $40,000. After accounting for inflation at 4% per year, you still have $20,000, or twice what you started with.

Understanding Investment Risk

The springboard to successful investing is balancing risk and reward.

If you want the rewards of successful investing—financial security and the sense of accomplishment that comes with mastering what may seem like a daunting adventure—you have to be willing to take some risks.

That doesn't mean you have to take flying leaps into untested waters. But it does mean you have to venture into growth investments, usually stocks and stock mutual funds. It may sound illogical, but the greatest risks novice investors face are concentrating too much on investment income and putting too much money into just a few investments.

HIGHER RISK

- Putting all your money in one investment
- Investing in products you don't understand
- Concentrating on investments that get eaten away by inflation
- Focusing on quick profits
- Investing money you cannot afford to lose in riskier ventures

- Putting money into newer, untried funds or companies
- Taking more risk with a small percentage of your portfolio
- Expanding your investment portfolio into new or different areas
- Allocating the largest portion of your portfolio to equities

- Investing in a balanced portfolio
- Selecting investments suited to meeting specific goals
- Emphasizing long-term growth
- Buying well-established mutual funds, stocks, or high-rated bonds

LOWER RISK

WHAT RISK MEANS

Though the biggest investment risk you take is doing nothing at all, the risk you may be most worried about is the possibility of losing your money.

With many investments, the risk of loss can be minimal. If you buy a ten-year U.S. Treasury bond when it is issued and keep it until it matures, you'll get back all the money you invested. Plus, you'll have earned ten years of interest.

Sometimes the risk of loss is greater because the investment may not live up to its promise. Buying stock in a start-up company, for example, increases your risk since, statistically, new ventures are more likely to fail than established ones.

While you'll need to take some risk if you're going to invest seriously, you can minimize it by **diversifying**, or spreading your investments around, a principle that's discussed later in this chapter.

STAYING TUNED IN

You can't avoid risk by making investments and then forgetting about them. You have to evaluate the performance of each investment separately, and be prepared to make adjustments to your portfolio, all the while sticking with your long-term investment plan. All the evidence suggests that starting early and staying with it are crucial to investment success. But individual investments can change in value, either because they

TIME IN THE MARKET

Investing isn't a competition, and you don't measure your score against anybody else's. But you can learn a lot about risk by measuring the results of one investment approach against the results of another.

The comparison below illustrates that consistent, long-term investing during an extended bull market paid big dividends to many investors. What's more, it shows that if you try to move in and out of the stock market to take advantage of the best opportunities and avoid the worst ones, you risk a dramatically inferior performance.

$10,000 AND HOW IT GREW, 1987–1997

All 10 years
$39,276

Miss 10 best days
$28,225

Miss 30 best days
$17,698

Miss 40 best days
$14,520

OppenheimerFunds, 1998

become riskier, provide lower returns, or because they no longer fit into your plan.

Suppose you put money into a global growth fund with holdings in both U.S. and overseas markets early in your investing career. As your equity portfolio grows, you might want to invest a larger percentage in other countries' equities. Or, you might consider moving your accumulated global fund assets into an international fund and building your U.S. investments separately.

THE RISK OF SAFETY

If you're so worried about the possibility of losing money that you put your money only into investments you consider absolutely safe—like insured CDs or U.S. Treasury bills—you're investing to **preserve principal**. Basically, that means you expect to get back what you put in, plus the interest you earn.

For many people, bank CDs seem the safest investments because they're FDIC-insured. Unlike other investments, where you risk losing money, most bank deposits, including CDs, are guaranteed by the Federal Deposit Insurance Corporation for up to $100,000 per customer. (Remember, though, that the insurance doesn't

cover other investments you buy at banks, including mutual funds and annuities.)

As an investment strategy, preservation of principal has its own serious risks. First, insured investments often pay less than uninsured investments. Then, the double blow of taxes and inflation steadily erodes your **real return**, or the purchasing power of what you get back in relation to what you invest.

Preservation of capital may be an appropriate short-term strategy. But over the long term, you should focus on growth.

Managing Risk

Risk won't take you by surprise if you know where and when to expect it.

The one thing about risk you can be fairly sure of is that it will pop up from time to time. But when you realize that risk is a normal part of investing, you can figure out ways to keep the lid on. In fact, you can come out ahead as a savvy investor by balancing the various risks you take to produce a potentially greater reward.

RISK TOLERANCE

Risk doesn't mean the same thing to everybody. That's because some people can live with—or can afford—more risk than others.

There's no way around the fact that most investments will drop in value at some point. That's what risk is all about. Knowing how to tolerate risk and avoid panic selling is part of a sound investment strategy.

For example, an aggressive growth mutual fund can be a smart way to build your long-term portfolio. But if you switch money out of this fund in a down period, you lose the potential increase in value. You may lose money as well.

You can build your tolerance—or compensate for it—in several ways:

1 Remember that over the long haul, taking some risk may increase reward

2 Take risks you can live with, by concentrating on stock and mutual fund investments with a stable history

3 Keep the bulk of your money in investments that don't require constant monitoring

4 Discuss any change in investment strategy with your financial advisor

BANG FOR YOUR BUCK

RISK ASSESSMENT

Risk is too complex to measure by any one standard. For example, there's the risk of not earning as much in one place as another, or having an investment do less well than you expected.

When you're trying to figure out how risky an investment could be, you have to factor in a number of different elements.

Management risk exists because the way a mutual fund, a corporation and even a government performs is often a reflection of the way it is managed. Change in management often signals a shift in strategy. Sometimes that can turn around an ailing company. Or, it might mean abandoning a formula that has worked well for years.

Currency fluctuations affect the value of your overseas investments. While having international holdings in your investment portfolio balances other risks, owning them means you're affected by changes in the value of that currency.

Political climates around the world influence the risks you face in making certain investments. A period of instability in an emerging market, for example, can drive the value of investments in that market down, while political stability and growth can increase value.

MARKET RISK

Market risk is what can happen in the stock and bond markets. If you invest in a profitable stock mutual fund, and the stock market declines, the value of the fund will drop. You might lose money if you have to sell at that point. If you wait until prices rebound and move upwards, you might avoid a loss.

RECESSION RISK

A **recession**, or period of economic slowdown, means investments of all kinds can lose value and make investing seem riskier. Of course, the opposite is true, too. Things seem less risky during periods of prosperity.

INTEREST RATE RISK

Interest rates create several potential risks. When interest rates go up, inflation increases. The price of your existing fixed-income investments, like bonds, declines since they're paying less than newly issued bonds. The money you're earning on those investments will buy less. Plus, higher rates may also mean that stock prices decline as investors put more money into interest-paying investments.

DUD

Time and Risk

Quick changes can speed you forward or take the wind out of your sails.

Volatility is the speed with which an investment gains or loses value. The more volatile it is, the more you can potentially make or lose in the short term. But in most cases, if you have a sense of the potential risk involved and the confidence to wait for prices to stabilize, you'll be prepared to ride out the storm.

For example, **equities** (specifically stocks and stock mutual funds) tend to change price more quickly than most **fixed-income** investments (bonds and bank deposits). But it's not always that simple. The price of stock in large, well-established companies tends to change more slowly than stock in smaller, or newer, companies. And the more predictable a company's business, the slower the price fluctuation is apt to be. You can compare the rapid changes in technology stocks, for example, with the relative stability in large-company stocks.

There are other factors to consider, too. Low-rated, high-yield bonds and some bond funds fluctuate in price at least as often as stocks, and offer some of the same opportunities for gain—and loss. That's one more reason for understanding the whole story on any investment you're considering.

TIME AND RISK

Volatility poses the biggest investment risk in the short term. If you wait out downturns in price, the chances are that an investment's value will rebound, and you can end up with a gain.

What's true for an individual investment is true for the market as a whole. Over the last 70 years, each major drop in the stock market—two market crashes and a half-dozen **bear markets**, when the value of stocks dropped 15% or more—has been followed by long-term recovery.

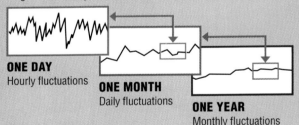

ONE DAY
Hourly fluctuations

ONE MONTH
Daily fluctuations

ONE YEAR
Monthly fluctuations

NO PAIN, NO GAIN

Illogical as it may seem, predictability is sometimes a bigger risk to your long-term investments than volatility.

The best example is what happens if you're wedded to safe-and-sound CDs—or other kinds of cash equivalent investments like money-market funds or U.S. Treasury bills. For example, suppose you'd kept your money in CDs in the five-year period beginning in 1990. A $1,000 investment would have been worth $1,270, a 5.4% annualized gain before taxes in 1995.

But had you weathered the same five years of ups and downs in the stock market with the same initial investment (tracked by the Dow Jones Equity Index), it would have been worth $2,222, an annualized gain of 24.4% before taxes. You find annualized gains by dividing the gain for the entire period by the number of years.

WATCHING THE MOVEMENT

If you recognize a certain trend in stock prices, you can turn it to your advantage. For example, some investments, known as **cyclicals**, move in identifiable patterns, up in certain economic climates and down in others.

If you invest when a cyclical stock is down and sell when it's up, you benefit from the movement. One problem, of course, is knowing when to get in and out. Your advisor can help you decide.

Other investments are more volatile and less predictable. For example, technology stocks (and the mutual funds that invest in them) jumped dramatically in value during 1995. But in the years before that many of them performed rather poorly.

If you look at the big picture, you'll discover that what seems to be a huge drop in price evens out when it is part of a longer-term pattern, as the illustration to the left demonstrates.

Another way to deal with volatility is to capitalize on it. If an equity increases dramatically in value, you can sell it and make another investment. Then, when the price of the equity you sold drops, you can buy it again and wait for the cycle to repeat itself. The one investment strategy that's pretty much doomed to failure is trying to **time the market**, or predict what the stock and bond markets are going to do next so you can be in the right place at the right time. The reason? It simply can't be done. Or at least nobody has been able to do it successfully over a period of time.

READING THE WIND

The range between an investment's high and low price over a period of time—often a year—is one measure of its volatility. The smaller the percentage of change the less volatile the investment.

In this excerpt from the stock pages of The Wall Street Journal, you can see that the price of Omnicare was more volatile than the price of Oneida during the previous 12 months. Omnicare ranged from 21⅛ to 54¾, or 159%, while Oneida ranged from 13⅜ to 17⅝, or 25%.

One strategy some investors use to avoid volatility is to sell stock when its price increases or drops a predetermined percent, often in the range of 10% to 20%. One way to handle this approach is to put in a **stop sell** order, instructions to your broker or advisor to sell any investment automatically when it drops below the level that you set.

VOLATILITY'S REWARDS

Don't get the mistaken impression that volatility is to be avoided at all costs. It can work in your favor at least as dramatically as it can work against you. In fact, a strong stock market often produces rapidly increasing prices in a relatively short time. That, in turn, can increase the value of your investment portfolio.

LARGE COMPANY STOCKS

U.S. TREASURY BILLS

UTILITY STOCKS

LEVELING OUT YOUR RISK

You can neutralize the impact of volatility with a buying strategy known as **dollar cost averaging**. Using this approach, you invest the same amount regularly in a specific investment, such as a mutual fund, paying whatever the going price is. When the price goes up, your dollars buy fewer shares. When it goes down, they buy more.

The effect, over time, can be to lower the cost of the average share of stock or mutual fund you buy, so that you end up with more shares for less money (see page 89).

Diversification

Investing, like a healthy diet, requires diversity and balance.

ONE MODEL OF DIVERSITY

If you woke up one morning $250,000 richer, how would you invest the money? Here's one hypothetical solution that could provide both diversity and balance. You should work out an appropriate model with your financial advisor.

If there were a single, perfect investment, your life as an investor would be a lot easier. But since it doesn't exist, the next best thing is to build your portfolio by balancing a variety of investments that together will help you achieve your goals. As a group, a portfolio of investments offsets the risks that any one investment might pose individually. That's what the principle of **diversification** is all about.

GROWTH INVESTMENTS

SPECIFIC INVESTMENTS

Step 3: Divide the money allocated to each level of risk among several different investments. You'll find plenty of choices with moderate risk.

Growth Fund

Blue Chip Stock

Emerging Market Fund

International Stock Fund

Stock

Equity Income Fund

Aggressive Growth Fund

Growth and Income Fund

Stock Fund

Stock

Balanced Fund

Speculative Stock

ALLOCATION

Step 2: Divide both growth and income investment into three parts—putting most into moderate-, some into low-, and the least into high-risk investments.

60% MODERATE RISK

30% LOWER RISK

10% HIGHER RISK

GROWTH VS. INCOME

Step 1: Decide how much to allocate to growth and how much to income.

70% GROWTH INVESTMENTS

TOTAL WORTH

Creating a diversified portfolio means putting money into a variety of investments following a well-thought out plan.

$250,00

DIVERSITY VS. CHAOS

You won't achieve diversity by buying impulsively when an investment sounds intriguing, or by increasing the sheer numbers of your investments. If you buy different investments randomly rather than striking a balance, you're more likely to create chaos than diversity.

Strange as it seems, diversity has to be planned with an eye to the present and the future.

For example, if you expect a substantial pension from your employer when you retire, you may not be as concerned with

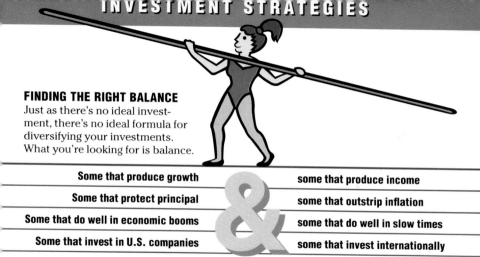

FINDING THE RIGHT BALANCE

Just as there's no ideal investment, there's no ideal formula for
diversifying your investments.
What you're looking for is balance.

Some that produce growth	&	some that produce income
Some that protect principal		some that outstrip inflation
Some that do well in economic booms		some that do well in slow times
Some that invest in U.S. companies		some that invest internationally

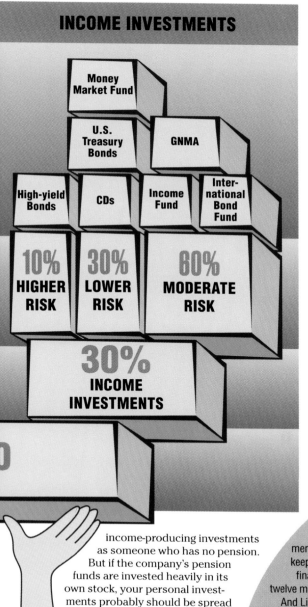

INCOME INVESTMENTS

Money Market Fund

U.S. Treasury Bonds

GNMA

High-yield Bonds

CDs

Income Fund

International Bond Fund

10% HIGHER RISK

30% LOWER RISK

60% MODERATE RISK

30% INCOME INVESTMENTS

UNTYING THE KNOT

Single-minded devotion has
no place in investing. While
it may be crucial to a personal relationship, loyalty
to an investment can end in
separation—your separa-
tion from financial security.
You're especially vulnerable if you concentrate all
of your money in one kind
of investment—the prover-
bial putting all your eggs in
one basket.

If all your money is in
bank CDs and money-
market mutual funds, for
example, you're limiting
yourself to lower-yielding,
income-producing invest-
ments that may lose the
battle with inflation.

But it's just as risky to
buy shares in a half-dozen
mutual funds that spe-
cialize in small-company
growth, or stocks in a
dozen pharmaceutical
companies—however
well they're doing at
the moment. The more
narrowly focused you are,
the more vulnerable you
are to changing market
conditions.

TOO MUCH OF A GOOD THING

While you can never have
too much invested, you can
own too many different investments. One clue is having a hard time
keeping track of what you have. Many
financial advisors suggest that six to
twelve mutual funds is a reasonable range.
And Lipper Analytical Services suggests
a goal of no more than 10% or less than 5%
of your total portfolio in any single fund.*

income-producing investments
as someone who has no pension.
But if the company's pension
funds are invested heavily in its
own stock, your personal investments probably should be spread
around among a broader range
of equity and debt.

Allocating Your Assets

Divide and conquer is the best way to win your investment battle.

In the end, **asset allocation**—the way you divide your portfolio among **stocks, bonds and cash**—has the greatest impact on reaching your financial goals. Stocks include stock mutual funds. Cash is usually invested in money market funds, CDs and Treasury bills.

Here's why asset allocation is such a critical principle of sound investing:

- **No single investment produces the best return year in and year out**
- **Stocks have historically turned in the strongest performance in most years and over the long term**
- **Bonds produce the best returns in some years**
- **Cash usually provides the weakest returns**

Therefore, you generally get the best long-term returns by putting the biggest share of your portfolio in stocks, the least in cash, and the rest in bonds.

AN AGGRESSIVE APPROACH*

80% STOCKS

15% BONDS
5% CASH

CREATING A FORMULA

As the evidence piles up on the importance of asset allocation, financial experts have devised some formulas that tend to work well over time.

Don't be confused if you encounter a range of suggested allocations. Brokerage firms, for example, modify their recommendations regularly, though rarely dramatically, in response to changes in the economy.

Any standard allocation can be modified to suit your own financial situation and your tolerance for risk. For example, you can decide on a single allocation model—say 60% in stocks, 30% in bonds

and 10% in cash—and stick with it. Or you may decide to modify your allocation over time, perhaps increasing your stock holdings to 80% earlier in your financial life, and reducing them to 40% after you retire.

Most advisors agree, though, that you probably ought to have a substantial holding in equities, basically mutual funds and stocks.

THROUGH THICK AND THIN

Seeing the wisdom of using an allocation model is the easy part. Sticking with it is often more difficult.

Let's say you divided your $10,000 portfolio into a 60%-30%-10% stock, bond and cash allocation a year ago. Since

WHAT A DIFFERENCE AN ALLOCATION MAKES

Asset allocation has a dramatic long-term impact, as you can see by comparing the pre-tax value of three hypothetical $100,000 portfolios after 20 years.* The first portfolio, emphasizing stocks, outperformed the portfolios with larger percentages allocated to bonds and cash.

The account values assume all earnings were reinvested, and are figured using the average annual returns for each investment category between 1926 and 1997: stocks at 11%, long-term government bonds at 5.2%, and cash at 3.7%

	Allocation	Value	Allocation	Value	Allocation	Value
Stocks	60%	$ 435,600	30%	$ 217,800	10%	$ 72,600
Bonds	30%	$ 78,900	60%	$ 157,800	30%	$ 78,900
Cash	10%	$ 19,900	10%	$ 19,900	60%	$ 119,400
Total		**$ 534,400**		**$ 395,500**		**$ 270,900**

Source: Ibbotson Associates, 1998**

then, the stock market has been booming, and the bond market has faltered. If you add up the value of your investments, your portfolio may have 75% of its value in stocks, 20% in bonds, and 5% in cash.

If you're committed to your strategy, you can either put new investment money into bonds and cash equivalents, to bring the value of your overall holdings back into balance. Or you might sell off some of your stock and buy bonds or Treasury bills with the proceeds to return to the original balance.

A MODERATE APPROACH*

60% STOCKS

30% BONDS

10% CASH

AN EASIER APPROACH

If juggling your investments to keep your allocation mix the way you want it seems complicated, there's an easier strategy. If you're using the moderate approach suggested above, for example, each time you have money to invest—say $1,000—you could put $600 into a stock mutual fund, $300 into a bond fund and $100 into a money-market fund toward the purchase of your next CD or T-bill.

While your overall portfolio may never be allocated as precisely as a hypothetical model, perfection isn't what you're after. But by adding money to all three investment categories, in the approximate proportions you've decided on, you've made asset allocation easier to keep on top of.

And remember, while it may seem smart to keep investing in stocks while they're hot, you may increase your risk over time by tampering with your asset allocation.

INTO THE FUTURE

It's just as important to allocate the investments in your retirement funds as it is to direct the money you're investing on your own. That means putting a substantial part of your 401(k) or IRA account, for example, into stocks and some into fixed-income investments, though probably little or nothing to cash.

And it also means looking at the bigger picture of your retirement and non-retirement investments together. For example, if you're putting most of your 401(k) money in growth mutual funds, you may want to balance that by putting a larger share of your nonretirement money into blue chip stocks.

Or, if you know you're eligible for a specific, fixed-income pension when you retire, you may want to invest more heavily in stocks on your own. Sorting out all the details and figuring out the best overall allocation is one of the ways working with your financial advisor may make a real difference to your bottom line.

A CONSERVATIVE APPROACH*

40% STOCKS

40% BONDS

20% CASH

ADDED FLAVORS

While stocks and bonds are the meat and potatoes of asset allocation, many financial advisors suggest adding a little spice. You could put some money in gold, some in real estate and part of your stock allocation in emerging growth companies.

Branching out can be an acquired taste, though. As you learn more about investing, and have more money to invest, you may decide you're ready for more adventure. Or you may prefer to draw the line at equity investments you're already comfortable with.

Figuring Your Return

The bright side of taking investment risks is reaping the rewards.

Successful investing is usually the result of making educated decisions and taking calculated risks. Nothing brings that winning combination into clearer focus than evaluating the **return**, or rewards, of your portfolio.

Total return, or the amount your investment increases in value, plus the earnings it pays, is the most accurate measure of an individual stock or mutual fund performance.

The best way to evaluate an investment's performance is by calculating **percentage return**, or total return divided by initial cost. And since the most accurate comparisons are on a yearly

basis, you can find the **annual percentage return** by dividing the percentage return by the number of years you've owned the investment.

Remember, though, that comparing returns as a way to decide which investments to keep and which to sell works best if you compare similar investments or investments with similar goals.

For example, if you compare the total return of one small-company stock fund with another fund investing in the same kinds of companies, you can tell which fund is performing better. The same is true for two bond funds, or other investments of the same type.

CALCULATING RETURN

When you invest for growth, as you do, for example, when you buy stocks and stock mutual funds, one measure of your success is the **return**, or the amount you get back, in comparison to what you invest. With a little calculation, you can use return figures to evaluate the performance of investments in relation to each other.

for example

In the hypothetical case used in this example, an investor bought 200 shares of a stock for $25 a share in January 1986 and sold it for $45 a share in December 1996, a gain of $20. The stock paid a steady dividend of $1.50 per share, or $300 a year.*

TOTAL RETURN

is the amount your investment increases in value plus the dividends it pays.

	Dividends
+	Gain in value
=	TOTAL RETURN

The information you need to figure your return is all part of your tax records.

	$3,000	($300 per year x 10 years)
+	**$4,000**	($20 per share x 200 shares)
=	**$7,000**	Total return

PERCENTAGE RETURN

is the total return divided by the cost of the investment.

	Total return
÷	Price of investment
=	PERCENTAGE RETURN

In an actual case, the gain in value would be reduced by the cost of commissions.

	$7,000	Total return
÷	**$5,000**	(200 shares @ $25 a share)
=	**140%**	Percent return

ANNUAL PERCENTAGE RETURN

is the percentage return divided by the number of years you held the investment. That's the number you need to make your comparisons.

	Percentage return
÷	Years you held investment
=	ANNUAL PERCENTAGE RETURN

When you're making long-term investments, an occasional decline in value can be offset by stronger performances in other years.

	140%	Percent return
÷	**10**	Years you held investment
=	**10.4%**	Annual percentage return

COMPARING RETURNS

Figuring out the actual return on your investments can be difficult. And you can't expect to compare the performance of different kinds of investments solely on their return. Here are some of the reasons:

- The amount and make-up of your investment changes. Most investment portfolios are active, with money moving in and out.

- The time you hold specific investments varies. When you buy or sell can have a dramatic effect on your overall return.

- The return on some investments—like real estate investments, zero-coupon bonds and limited partnerships—is difficult to pin down, partly because they're more difficult to liquidate easily. You have to evaluate them by different standards, including their tax advantages.

- The method of computing return on different investments may vary. For example, performance can be averaged or compounded, which changes the rate of return dramatically.

HOW MUCH IS ENOUGH?

How much return do investors expect? It changes over time, if the market price of stocks is any indication. One explanation seems to be that investors demand returns on their equity investments that beat the yields on long-term government bonds. As the interest rate drops, investors seem willing to pay more for stocks than they would when bond yields are high.

KEEPING UP TO DATE

You don't have to wait until you sell an investment to get a sense of the kind of return you're getting. If you're tracking a stock's performance, total return isn't reported in the press, but you can use the current price of the stock to estimate your unrealized gain in value. (It's unrealized because you still own the stock. When you sell, you realize the gain.) Then use the formula on the opposite page, just as you would if you'd sold.

If you're tracking mutual fund performance, you can find updated information on every fund's total return—which includes dividends and increases in value—regularly in the financial pages of your newspaper, in magazines or on-line using the Internet's World Wide Web or commercial software.

Your financial advisor, the brokerage firm where you have an account or your mutual fund company also may include information on the return of various investments in your portfolio in their monthly, quarterly or annual reports. If they don't provide what you want to know, you can ask for it.

> **You can compare your return to the performance of different benchmarks**

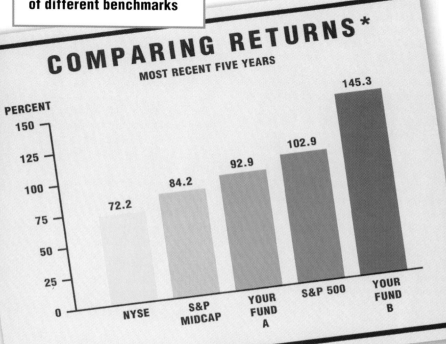

COMPARING RETURNS*
MOST RECENT FIVE YEARS

PERCENT

- NYSE: 72.2
- S&P MIDCAP: 84.2
- YOUR FUND A: 92.9
- S&P 500: 102.9
- YOUR FUND B: 145.3

Searching for Yield

Yield measures your investment income against the price you paid.

If you're earning $600 a year on a money market fund in which you invested $10,000 and another $600 on a savings account with a balance of $20,000, you should be aware that the first investment is doing twice as well as the second.

The difference between the two is the **yield**, or what you're making on your investment. Even though the income from each is the same, you need twice as much in the savings account to produce the equivalent amount. That's because you're earning 3% on your savings, but 6% on the money fund. If all your money were in an investment yielding 6%, your income would be $1,800 rather than $1,200, or 50% more.

When It's Simple...

You figure yield by dividing the amount you receive annually in interest or dividends by the amount you spent to buy the investment.

For example, if you spend $1,000 on a bond and get $60 in annual interest, the yield is 6% [$60 ÷ $1,000 = 6%]. And if you hold onto the bond until it matures, you'll go on collecting a 6% yield until you redeem the bond and get your $1,000 back.

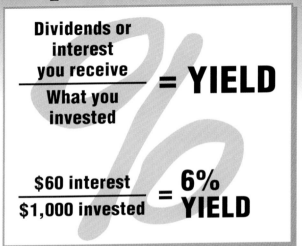

$$\frac{\text{Dividends or interest you receive}}{\text{What you invested}} = \textbf{YIELD}$$

$$\frac{\$60 \text{ interest}}{\$1,000 \text{ invested}} = \frac{6\%}{\textbf{YIELD}}$$

TIME AND YIELD

The yield that's reported in the stock and bond pages of the financial section of the newspaper is actually **current yield**, or what you're receiving in relation to the current price of the investment. For U.S. Treasury bonds and notes, the current yield is reported as **ask yield**, or the yield based on the price that sellers are asking for the bond.

You'll also sometimes hear about a bond's **yield to maturity**, a more accurate estimate of what it will be worth to you over time. It's figured using a complex formula involving the interest rate, the price you paid, the par value and the years to maturity. Although it's rarely reported in bond tables, you can ask your financial advisor for the information.

If you have a bond that you bought when it was issued, and intend to hold until it matures, you don't have to worry about current yield. But if you're thinking about buying or selling bonds, current yield is one way to estimate what you'll get back on your investment.

YIELD DOLLARS AND SENSE

Paying attention to yield is smart, since it is a measure of how well you're doing in building your assets. But there are some danger zones:

- Small differences in yield are usually not worth chasing, unless you have large amounts invested. The extra $25 you'd make moving a $10,000 CD from a local bank paying 5% to one across the country paying 5.25% could easily get spent on phone calls and postage

- Yield alone does not tell you as much about how well an equity investment is performing as total return does

- Risky investments promising high yields may be okay in small doses, but as a regular diet, they can be big trouble. That's especially true with most **derivatives**, or investments whose values depend entirely on the way other investments are performing

YORK EXCHANGE BOND

CORPORATION BONDS
Volume, $16,714,000

Bonds	Cur Yld	Vol	Close	Net Chg.
Chiquta 10½04	10.1	35	103⅞	+ ⅛
ChckEul 7s12	cv	1	84	+ 1
Chrslr 10.4s99	9.8	18	105⅞	+ ⅛
CINVE 6⅝s01		5	101⅛	+ ⅞
Clardge 11¾02	12.5	299	94	− ⅛
ClevEl 8¼05	9.0	25	97½	+ ⅞
ClevEl 9¼09	9.3	25	100	+ ¼
ClevEl 8⅜11	9.1	75	92	...
ColeWld zr13	...	8	34	− ¼
CmlCr 8s96	7.9	43	101	− ¼
CmwE 7⅝s03F	7.6	5	100⅛	− 1⅛
CmwE 7⅝s03J	7.5	10	101½	+ ⅝

Bonds
LgIsLt 7.3s99
LgIsLt 8.9s19
LgIsLt 9¾21
LgIsLt 9s22
LgIsLt 8.2s
LgIsLt 9s9
Malan 9½
MarO 7s0
Masco
Mascot
Maxus
viMcC
McD
M

CHANGING YIELDS

Yield changes when the price of an investment changes. For example, the Chrysler bond paying 10.4% interest is currently yielding only 9.8% because the price is $1,058.75 (105⅞), or $58.75 (5⅞) above par. In contrast, the Claridge bond paying 11.75% interest is currently yielding 12.5% because the bond is selling for $940 (94), or $60 below par.

When It's Not So Simple...

The life of an investor isn't always simple, and neither is figuring yield, especially if you're trying to evaluate the performance of an investment that:

- **Changes in price**
- **Pays no interest or dividends until sold**
- **Earns interest at anything other than a straight annual rate**

INTEREST Vs. YIELD

It's easy to confuse the interest rate an investment is paying with its yield, since they're both stated as a percentage of the amount of the investment. To complicate matters further, there are times when they are the same. The best examples are CDs that pay simple interest and bonds that you buy at **par value**, or the price at

ONE YEAR CD
ANNUAL PERCENTAGE YIELD **6.25%**
INTEREST RATE **6.00%**

which they are issued. Then a 6% rate means a 6% yield.

However, if interest is **compounded** (added to your balance), or if the price of a bond moves higher or lower than par, the yield will be different than the interest rate. Of the two, yield is the one that matters when it comes to figuring out how well you're doing with your investments.

STEPPING UP YOUR STRATEGY

When interest rates are high, as they were during the early 1980s, it's easy to get used to strong yields on even the most conservative investments. But what happens when a 5-year CD that's been yielding 10% matures, and the best you can find is one yielding 5%?

One solution for many fixed-income investments—specifically CDs and bonds—is to use a technique known as **laddering**. Instead of putting $30,000 in a single 10-year bond, you can buy three bonds, each worth $10,000, that mature two years apart.

Each time one matures, you reinvest that amount. That way, if you have to settle for a lower rate for that part of your money, you'll still be earning the higher rate on the rest. And when the next bond matures, the rates may be up again.

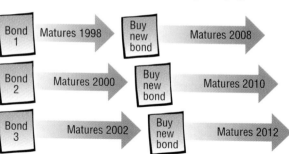

Bond 1	Matures 1998	Buy new bond	Matures 2008
Bond 2	Matures 2000	Buy new bond	Matures 2010
Bond 3	Matures 2002	Buy new bond	Matures 2012

Setting and Meeting Your Goals

If you know where you want to go, you can plan the route and set the pace to get there.

"I know I want to own my own home."

THE FIRST STEP IN BUYING A HOUSE IS HAVING ENOUGH MONEY FOR A DOWN PAYMENT

Most buyers need between 10% and 20% of the purchase price of a house to use as a down payment before they can consider buying.

OTHER GOALS

Your financial goals don't have to be limited to fulfilling major responsibilities, even though you may focus most of your investment dollars on a few essentials. One of the challenges of choosing among competing goals is deciding which are most important to you, and how you can afford them without losing sight of your priorities. Your list might include:

 Wedding

 Travel

 Family celebrations

 Car

 Hobby

"I know I want to give my kids a good _education_."

TO PAY FOR A COLLEGE EDUCATION, INVESTMENTS MUST GROW FASTER THAN THE INFLATION RATE

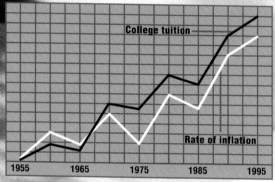

College tuition

Rate of inflation

1955   1965   1975   1985   1995

By starting now, you can begin to build the investment portfolio you need to pay tuition.

"I know I want to be comfortable in _retirement_."

WOMEN NEED TO GO THE EXTRA MILE TO SAVE FOR RETIREMENT

After you retire, you'll need income you can depend on to meet your expenses. No one source alone is likely to supply it. How much can you count on from each one of these standard sources?

Social Security   Pension   Part-time jobs   Investment income

Investment income can increase over time, so it will play a big role in your long-term security.

Creating a Timetable

Knowing *when* you'll need the money for specific goals helps you plan *how* to get it.

When you're planning for the things you expect to happen, predictability is an asset, not a liability. That's especially true with many of the goals that are most important to you—perhaps owning your own home, enjoying a secure retirement, or paying for college. In fact, you not only expect them to happen, but you have a pretty good idea of when you'll need the money to pay for them.

Since these are ambitions many women share, planning for them puts you in good company. It means that as you begin to choose investments to meet those goals, you can benefit from what others have learned about getting your priorities in order, balancing competing demands and selecting the right places to put your money to work.

SHORT TERM

- Furthering your education
- Buying a new car
- Buying a home
- Opening a business
- Starting an investment portfolio

MID-TE

LONG

WHAT IF YOU DON'T PLAN?

If you sometimes think that what you want out of life is so normal that it will just happen in the regular course of events, you're being lulled by a false sense of security. Most financial advisors agree that goals become realities only when you have invested enough to make them happen.

Ask yourself, for instance, if you'd have enough money for a down payment if your ideal house were for sale right now. Or, whether you'd be able to pay a $20,000 tuition bill if your child had just

been accepted to college. If your answer is yes, you can breathe more easily. But if it's no, then this is the time to act.

To have money available when you need it, you have to develop a plan for making the kinds of investments that are most likely to produce what you'll need. For example, most financial advisors agree that long-term goals require regular investment in growth equities (see pages 44–45). Identifying what those investments are, learning how to put money into them—and then doing it—is precisely what planning for the future is all about.

COMPETING FOR YOUR DOLLARS

In many cases, your goals will be competing with each other for your investment dollars. By planning ahead, you can develop strategies for resolving the conflicts without having to abandon your goals along the way.

For example, if you start a retirement savings plan when you begin your career, you will accumulate the greatest amount by contributing part of every paycheck to your savings, year in and year out. Even if you miss a year or two, when you're buying a house, or paying college tuition, for instance, the money you've already invested will continue to grow. And when you begin contributing again, you won't be starting at ground zero.

Another strategy is to put aside specific income for specific purposes. For example, you might put any bonuses or extra-job income into an investment account set aside for one particular goal, like making home improvements or taking a special trip.

ADJUSTING YOUR GOALS TO FIT YOUR LIFE STYLE

Chances are your financial goals will shift over time, as your circumstances and priorities change. If you're just starting a career, for instance, getting the extra education you need to move ahead is probably at the top of your list. But if you marry and have a child, you might add a house and a college fund to your goals.

Setting up a timetable doesn't mean you're locked into anything. In fact, you should plan to revise your approach regularly—probably once a year.

- Paying children's tuition
- Expanding a business
- Buying a second home
- Building your investment portfolio
- Taking early retirement

- Saving for a comfortable retirement
- Setting up children's careers
- Pursuing special interests
- Caring for a family member

THE IMPACT OF TIME

Timing is an important part of financial planning. If you identify when you'll need investment income, you can select the investments designed to produce it at the right time.

For example, if you're 25, and retirement is 40 or more years away, most advisors recommend that you invest in growth equities. On the other hand, if you're 65 and about to retire, some of your investments perhaps should be geared to producing part of the income you'll need to live comfortably for the rest of your life.

The reality is, though, that you and most other women don't live by a fixed schedule. You might be 20 or 40 when your child is born, 30 or 50 when you settle into your career, 55 or 70 when you decide to retire. So *your* short-term concerns might be another woman's long-term plans, or vice versa. As long as you understand the role that time plays in the way most investments perform, you can make the best choices to suit your short- and long-term goals.

#1

To Buy or Not to Buy?

That may be the question. The answer is not easy when you think of your home as an investment.

If you're planning to buy a home, you probably have good reasons for your decision. It may be that you share many other people's feelings about being part of the American dream. But there are also financial issues involved in buying real estate that you need to consider as well.

From one perspective, a home is an investment, maybe the single largest one you'll ever make.

Like certain other investments, real estate has the potential to increase in value over the years, so that you can sell it for more than you paid.

But unlike investing in equities such as stock or mutual funds, which you buy as a way to achieve your financial goals, most people consider owning a home as an end in itself.

FOR SALE

REASONS TO BUY

Sometimes a buyer can simply pay cash to buy a home, but most people don't— even if they have enough money. One reason is that the interest on a mortgage is tax-deductible—one of the few ways you can reduce your taxable income and save on what you owe Uncle Sam.

If your accountant or financial advisor suggests you buy a home, that's often the reason. If you were making the same-sized mortgage payment as you had been paying in rent, you'd actually end up with more cash in your pocket, especially in the early years when you're paying a greater proportion of interest.

While it's not strictly financial, another advantage of buying a home is that you can usually get more space for your dollar than you do when you rent—sometimes a lot more.

REASONS TO RENT

On the other hand, you might decide to rent rather than buy a home for practical and financial reasons.

If you're on your own, for example, getting together a down payment, and managing the expense of a mortgage, taxes, insurance and upkeep may put too great a strain on your budget. And having all your assets tied up in your home has serious drawbacks. Among other things, it limits your ability to invest enough to meet the other goals that are important to you.

Another reason to rent is a job that keeps you on the move, or requires you

LACK OF LIQUIDITY IS ONE OF THE MAJOR PROBLEMS WITH INVESTING IN REAL ESTATE

to relocate periodically. It's not always easy to sell when you're transferred or change jobs. While your employer may help out with the cost of selling one place and buying another, you can't count on it. And the most expensive part of buying is the one-time, up-front costs.

FAMILY GIFTS

If your parents or grandparents are willing to help you out with buying a home, each of them can give you a tax-free gift of up to $10,000 a year (in 1998). It's a case where a timely gift may make a lot more sense than an inheritance.

Be careful, though. Gifts over the limit are taxable for the giver. And loans, even from family members, earn **imputed interest**. That means that even if the person who lends you the money doesn't charge you interest, he or she has to pay income tax on the interest that normally would be earned. One exception is when a parent's loan enables a child with no investment income to buy a home.

HOW BUYING WORKS

There are usually three distinct phases in buying a house: accumulating the down payment, finding a mortgage, and building your equity.

1 Generally you need a **down payment**, at least 10% and sometimes as much as 20% of the purchase price available in cash in order to buy. You can also investigate some federal and state programs, like those run by the Federal Housing Administration (FHA), which require a smaller amount up front. Your attorney or real estate agent should be able to tell you about special programs.

2 When you have enough for a down payment, you can begin looking for a mortgage. A **mortgage** is a long-term loan that provides you with the money you need to buy the home. You pay the loan back, usually in monthly installments over a 15- to 30-year period.

3 When you've arranged your mortgage and bought your home, you gradually build your **equity**, or ownership, by paying off the mortgage. In most cases your monthly payment will also include enough to cover the real estate taxes and insurance on the property.

INVESTING FOR A DOWN PAYMENT

If you're planning to buy your first home, you'll have to decide how to invest the money you're using for a down payment.

Timing is a major consideration. The sooner you plan to move, the fewer risks you may want to take. You probably don't want to be in a position to sell investments if their price drops suddenly, or risk having to postpone your plans. On the other hand, the more price-stable an investment is, the less you'll earn on it (see pages 98–99).

One technique advisors suggest is to split up the money you have accumulated, part in growth mutual funds and stocks, and the balance in interest-bearing investments that will mature when you plan to buy.

You could also set goals for the growth investments, say a 20% gain in price, and sell each time an investment reaches that level. That's a different approach from long-term investing, where equities grow in value over many years. But it could help you to build your down payment more quickly.

GENDER ISSUES

If you're single, it may be harder to get a mortgage than if you're married, and harder than if you were a single man. While it's illegal to discriminate based on age , race, or gender, a lender can always turn you down.

Sometimes you can make out better applying to a bank or credit union you already have a relationship with, or using a mortgage broker who specializes in finding interested lenders. You might also consider a private arrangement with sellers who are eager to get rid of their property—although you don't want to do that without the advice of a real estate lawyer you trust.

Qualifying for a Mortgage

The path to a mortgage isn't always a straight line, even when you have good directions.

You can get a mortgage from regular commercial banks, savings banks, credit unions and mortgage banks (also called mortgage loan companies). If you already have an account with a bank or credit union, you should check there first to see if you qualify for a preferred rate. However, it usually pays to shop around before you apply. The lowest rates and quickest approvals are often available from mortgage loan companies.

You probably won't know the exact interest rate you'll pay on your mortgage before you sign the final papers, though you may be able to lock in the rate that's available on the day you apply. That assurance may be a deciding factor in selecting the lender.

If your initial application is rejected, or if you aren't sure how to find a lender, you might decide to work with a **mortgage broker**, a person whose job it is to match you with a lender.

APPLY HERE

1 Package your financial information, putting your assets and liabilities in the best possible light. Regular employment, little debt, good credit and an investment portfolio can help.

As a general rule, you can afford to buy a house that costs up to 2½ times your annual income.

WHAT LENDERS WANT TO SEE

Lenders evaluate your application to decide if you're a good investment risk for them. In most cases, they use criteria set by the Government National Mortgage Association (GNMA). Here's an overview of the things those criteria require:

- No more than 28% of your total income needed to pay mortgage, insurance and taxes.
- A good credit record. Loan defaults, including any on student loans, are a problem.
- No more than 36% of your total income needed to pay your mortgage plus debts. Very large credit card balances can be a problem.
- The longer you've worked and the higher your salary, the better your chances.

2 Look for the lowest rate mortgage you can afford to reduce the interest you'll owe.

MORTGAGE RATES

The rate of interest you'll have to pay on your mortgage is determined primarily by the general interest rates at the time you borrow. When they're low, you pay less. And if they're high, you pay more. Both the rate you pay, and the **term**, or length, of your loan make a big difference in what it will cost you to buy.

This chart gives you a quick sense of the difference a rate makes on the monthly payment of a 30-year fixed-rate $125,000 mortgage:

Interest rate	6%	8%	10%	12%
Monthly payment	$749	$917	$1,097	$1,285

3 Decide which is more important: fixed payments or a lower initial rate. That will help you choose the type of mortgage.

MORTGAGE TYPES

Most lenders offer both fixed-rate and adjustable-rate mortgages. With a **fixed-rate mortgage**, the amount of interest you owe is set when you borrow because the rate stays the same over the length of the loan. With an **adjustable-rate mortgage**, the interest rate, and amount of interest you pay, rises or falls as interest rates in general move up or down.

The appeal of a fixed-rate loan is that you know what your housing expenses will be, so you can plan your budget more easily. But an adjustable-rate is usually cheaper initially, so it is easier to qualify for.

You can sometimes find a hybrid mortgage at a lower rate than a regular fixed-rate loan, which lets you plan your costs for the first few years. The most appealing have fixed rates for three, five or seven years, and then adjust every year. You'll need to discuss your choices with your lender or financial advisor to select the one that's best for you.

You'll also need 5% to 10% of your new home's cost in cash to close the deal.

FIXED
ADJUSTABLE
PRIME

4 Don't focus more on getting things done easily. Focus on getting a good deal on your mortgage.

MORTGAGE SHORTCUTS

The usual approach is to find the property you want and then go looking for a mortgage. But sometimes, when lenders have mortgage money available, they may offer you a chance to **prequalify**. That means you apply for a mortgage before you have chosen a home to buy. The lender will let you know how much you can borrow—or whether you'll qualify at all.

It's probably worth doing if you're serious about buying, since you can shop with more confidence if you know how much you can afford. But there's usually an application fee, so it's not something you want to do lightly.

Another way to simplify buying is to look at new construction rather than buy from a previous owner. Sometimes a builder is able to negotiate with a lender for lower rates or quicker approval than you could get on your own. But always check first to be sure it is the best deal you can get.

5 Work with a real estate lawyer to be sure you don't miss any important details about what you owe or the terms of repayment.

6 If you're turned down for a mortgage, insist on an explanation of the reasons.

EXTRA HELP

Mortgage research firms, like HSH Associates, provide a list of lenders and current rates in your area for a small fee. Their phone number is 800-873-2837. If you know what the going rates are, you'll be able to make better informed choices—and maybe get a better deal.

APPROVED

Building Equity

As you gradually pay off your mortgage, you own a bigger share of your home.

3

When you buy a home and make a down payment, you have **equity**, or a percentage of ownership, in the house. However, the equity you have can vary as you pay off your mortgage loan and the value of the house changes with market conditions.

VALUE OF HOME
− OUTSTANDING LOANS
= YOUR EQUITY

for example

	$ 200,000	Value of home
−	$160,000	Outstanding loans
=	$ 40,000	Total equity

For example, when you buy a $200,000 home with a $160,000 mortgage, your equity is 20% ($40,000 of $200,000 = 20%). When you make your final payment, your equity is 100% of its market value at the time.

Growing equity in your home improves your financial security in several ways. It means that if you want to buy a more expensive house you'll be able to make a larger down payment. You'll also have a larger net worth—and fewer liabilities—if you want to borrow. And when the mortgage is paid off, you'll have extra cash for other living expenses—plus a place to call your own.

CHANGING PROPERTY VALUES

The value of your equity changes when the market value of your home changes. For example, suppose a house you bought for $200,000—with $40,000 down and a $160,000 mortgage—is sold for $300,000. Your equity is now worth $140,000 plus any principal payment, because the amount you owe the lender ($160,000) is fixed. The rest is yours.

However, the reverse could be true, though it happens less often. For example, if you had a $160,000 mortgage on a home you bought for $200,000 but sold for $160,000, you would owe it all to the lender.

Your equity

As you pay your mortgage, you build your equity

LOOK BEFORE YOU LEAP

While home equity loans can solve short-term financial needs, you should consider the potential drawbacks as well as the advantages.

- **You reduce your equity by borrowing against the value of your home**
- **If you fall behind on repayment, you could risk losing your home even if you make your mortgage payments on time**
- **Since most home equity loans have adjustable interest rates, the cost of borrowing could increase**

HOME EQUITY LOANS

Having equity in your home means you may be eligible for a **home equity loan**, one of the easiest and most economical ways to borrow money. The application is similar to a mortgage application, but because your home serves as **collateral**, or security, for the loan, the process usually moves more quickly and costs you less in fees.

The amount you can borrow is influenced by a number of factors, including how much you owe on your mortgage and the lender's appraisal of your home's current value. Generally speaking, you can borrow up to 80% of your equity although some home equity loans have a **ceiling**, or upper limit, of $50,000.

Home equity loans have an advantage over personal loans, too, because the

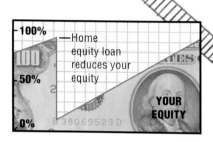

interest you pay is tax-deductible in most circumstances. While loans over $100,000 must usually be spent on actual improvements to your home, loans in smaller amounts can be used to pay your children's college tuition, or for a variety of purposes. Be sure to check with your tax advisor first, though, to avoid any problems.

TRADING UP

Once you've bought your first home, it's generally easier to buy another one, for two reasons: a credit history and more money to invest. If you've made regular mortgage payments, you've established a good credit record. And if you make a profit when you sell, you'll have more money for a new down payment. That will let you buy a more expensive home, or borrow less money—or both.

You can plan to trade up by starting with a modest home, perhaps improving it, and selling when you can make a profit.

This can be risky—prices can drop, mortgage rates can rise, people can hate the paint you picked out. But often it works just fine.

The tax code also works in your favor when you sell one home and buy another. That's because you don't have to pay any tax on your **capital gains**, or profit, on the sale of up to $500,000 if you're married and $250,000 if you're single. The only conditions are that you have lived in the home for at least two of the previous five years, and that at least two years pass before you use the exemption again.

The Cost of College

Whether you think of it as a goal, or as an investment in your child's future, a college education is expensive.

If you have children who'll be heading to college, take a look at the chart below. It projects what an education will cost for the next generation of students. When you can breathe again, it's time to start thinking about what you can do now.

The bottom line is that the sooner you develop a college investment strategy that's designed to accumulate the amount you'll need for tuition, the less strain college costs will place on your family budget when your child enrolls.

HOW MUCH YOU HAVE TO INVEST

To afford the cost of your child's college education, it's important to start investing right away. The estimated numbers below give you a sense of what you're working toward.

Years until student begins college	School year (fall)	Projected total 4-year cost		Monthly savings required	
		Public	Private	Public	Private
1	1998	$ 45,569	$ 96,957	$ 3,637	$ 7,738
2	1999	47,847	101,805	1,826	3,899
3	2000	50,239	106,895	1,231	2,619
4	2001	52,751	112,240	930	1,978
5	2002	55,389	117,852	749	1,593
6	2003	58,158	123,745	628	1,336
7	2004	61,066	129,932	541	1,151
8	2005	64,120	136,428	476	1,012
9	2006	67,326	143,250	425	904
10	2007	70,692	150,412	384	817
11	2008	74,226	157,933	350	745
12	2009	77,938	165,830	322	685
13	2010	81,835	174,121	298	634
14	2011	85,926	182,827	277	590
15	2012	90,223	191,968	259	551
16	2013	94,734	201,567	243	517
17	2014	99,470	211,645	229	487
18	2015	104,444	222,228	216	460

Note: Cost figures assume 5% annual increases and use College Board survey data for the current school year as a base. Savings figures assume investments yield 8% annually until the student enters college, at which point saving, and investment income, cease.

Source: T. Rowe Price Associates Inc.

MONEY WELL SPENT

A college education is usually a smart investment. A 1994 study by The U.S. Bureau of the Census showed that someone with an undergraduate degree has the potential to earn $600,000 more over his or her lifetime than someone without a college education. And in an increasingly technological age, most experts believe that difference is likely to increase.

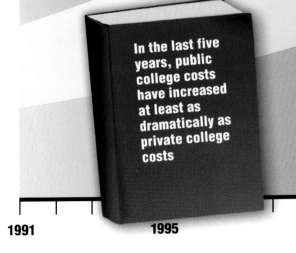

In the last five years, public college costs have increased at least as dramatically as private college costs

YEAR   1991   1995

A REAL CRUNCH

You'll probably need more money in a shorter period of time to pay for college than you will for anything else—with the possible exception of setting up a new business. And, if the past is any indicator, college costs will continue to go up.

In the last few years, increases have averaged 6% to 8% a year, roughly double the rate of inflation. Though there are some indications the rate of increase may be slowing, the actual dollar amount will continue to go up. And, in general, the most prestigious institutions are the most expensive.

Your child may qualify for scholarships or be eligible for loans, but colleges consider the costs of education primarily the parents' responsibility and expect you to be able to pay them.

COST OF 4 YEARS OF COLLEGE

TOP PRIVATE COLLEGES
are the most expensive but may offer the most aid

PRIVATE COLLEGES
try to attract outstanding students from all financial backgrounds

PUBLIC COLLEGES
are usually the least expensive but may offer little aid

$275,000

$250,000

$225,000

$200,000

$175,000

$150,000

$125,000

$100,000

$75,000

$50,000

$25,000

$0

2000   2005   2010

College Investing Primer

Learning the ABC's of investing can move you to the head of the class.

2

If there's college tuition in your future, you need to create an investment strategy to cover the cost. The longer you delay putting an investment plan into place, the greater the likelihood you'll face the prospect of having to borrow large sums or limiting your child's college choices.

AN INVESTMENT PRIMER

They're not quite as simple as ABC, but here are some frequently suggested ways to approach investing for college.

1 **Establish education accounts, separate from any other investment accounts**

2 **Add money every month**

3 **Choose investments based on your children's ages, stressing growth in the early years and safety as they get closer to 18**

INVESTMENTS TO AVOID

There are a number of investments that don't usually work very well as ways to invest for college savings, either because they're too aggressive or not aggressive enough. Or they may be hard to cash in when you most need them. They include:

- Any investment that doesn't pay enough interest to beat the rate of inflation, including savings accounts, short-term bond funds, money-market funds and similar investments.

- Any bonds you'll have to sell before they mature; the price fluctuates, so you could lose money.

- Any investment that's not easily liquidated, like real estate, unit investment trusts, and limited partnerships.

- Any derivatives, which are investments whose value depends entirely on the way some other investment performs, usually within a specific period of time.

- Any investment that would cost you surrender fees and taxes if you liquidated them, like annuities or IRAs.

When your children are young, most financial advisors would urge investing primarily in equities, stocks and stock mutual funds. If you reinvest all the earnings or use them to make similar investments, the value of your portfolio should grow.

THE VALUE OF EQUITIES

Most experts agree that investments which grow in value—stock and mutual funds in particular—are the right choices for meeting expenses that are constantly increasing. You can get all the advantages of equity investing, and limit potential risks, by starting a college fund when each child is born. And you can minimize taxes by making growth investments, which usually don't produce much current income.

A BIG CHOICE

There are about 3,600 degree-granting institutions in the U.S.—including universities, four-year colleges and two-year colleges. About half are public, which means they're supported by state or local governments, and the rest are private.

THE NAME ON THE ACCOUNT

Should you put investments earmarked for college in your child's name instead of your own? There are two arguments in favor of this—that you'd be less apt to spend the money for something else, and that your child might owe less tax on the money the investments earned. But there are several strong arguments against this practice:

- Children under 14 pay tax at their parent's rate, so there is no tax advantage for children this age

- Once you put money in a child's name, you give up the right to use it; and at 18 (21 in some states) the child can spend it as he or she wishes

- If you are planning to apply for financial aid, a child is expected to contribute a higher percentage of his or her assets than you are of yours (35% vs. 5.65%)

As they get older you may want to begin switching some of your port- folio into more price-stable investments, including equity income funds and medium-term Treasury bonds. If stock prices increase sharply, you might also sell some of your invest- ments to protect your gains. But you'll still benefit from growth.

TIMING IT RIGHT

There are some investments you can time, like the dates your CDs and Treasury bills come due. Since you'll need a cash transfusion, usually in August and January when the new semesters start, you can plan to have the money available then. Colleges usually require payment in full when students register.

When you're buying zero-coupon bonds, it's especially important to buy those that mature during the four- or five-year period that you'll need the cash. If you have to sell them before they're due, you may take a real beating on the price. And if you're buying U.S. Series EE Savings Bonds, remember that you have to keep them at least five years to collect the full interest.

As your child gets closer to college and actually enrolls, you may want to include more income-producing investments, and continue to transfer part of your equity assets gradually, some of them each year. The schedule should be dictated by when your tuition bills come due, not by what you think the market's going to do. But, if the stock market goes way up at any point in this period, you may want to take advan- tage of selling when the prices are high. In other words, you may want to speed up— but just a bit—the shift from stocks and mutual funds to more stable investments.

CATCHING THE LOWER RATE

One way to take advantage of your child's potentially lower tax rate is to make a gift of stocks or stock mutual funds to the child just before they're sold to pay college tuition. Since your child, not you, is selling the investment, the taxes on the profits could be less. And you won't owe any gift tax if the value of the stock or stock fund is $10,000 or less ($20,000 if two givers are involved).

Applying for Aid

You've got to be prepared to put in some time and effort.

#3

DUE JANUARY 1

To apply for financial aid, you must fill out a Free Application for Federal Student Aid (FAFSA). In addition, some colleges—about 400 at last count—also require you to complete a Financial Aid Profile if you want assistance from the school itself. Your child's high school guidance office and the college admissions office can tell you which forms you'll need and how to get them.

Both forms are due on January 1 of the year for which you're requesting aid—generally the January of your child's senior year in high school and each following January until the senior year of college.

The catch is—as anyone who's been through this can tell you—the forms are complicated and extremely probing. (Some people would even describe them as intrusive.) But there's virtually no way around filling them out if you want financial aid. As far as the colleges and the government are concerned, this is one place where privacy doesn't count.

Free Application for
1996-97 School Year

WARNING: If you purposely give false or misleading information on this form, you may be fined $10,000, sent to prison, or both.

Print in capital with a dark ink

Section A: You (the student)

1. Last name — SHORT

1–3. Your name
Your title (optional) — Mr.

4–7. Your permanent mailing address (All mail will be sent to this address. See Instructions, page 2 for state/country abbreviations.)
4. Number and street — 987 M
5. City — MYTOU

8. Your social security number (SSN) (Don't leave blank. See Instructions, page 2.) — 9876

FINANCIAL AID FORMULAS

There's a standard formula, known as Congressional Methodology, for figuring how much you're able to contribute to your child's education, and whether your family qualifies for federal financial aid. The Department of Education sends you a Student Aid Report (SAR) within a month of your application, stating your Expected Family Contribution (EFC). Colleges use that figure to determine the aid you are eligible for.

The amount your family is expected to contribute remains constant, regardless of the cost of the school. For example, if your contribution is set at $8,000, that could pay the entire cost at some public colleges. But it covers barely a quarter of the cost at the most expensive private schools.

The computation takes a number of factors into account:

- **Your income, including nontaxable income and money contributed to IRAs and Keogh plans (though not money invested in employer-sponsored retirement plans)**

- **Your assets, if your taxable income is more than $50,000; the value of your family's home isn't included, nor is money in retirement accounts and annuities**

- **Your child's earnings, investments and savings**

- **Your family's size and the number of people in college at the same time**

WHOSE INCOME COUNTS?

Parents are considered responsible for their children's education. If you and your child's father are separated or divorced, most private colleges require financial information from both of you before your child can be eligible for aid. And if you or your former husband have remarried, step-parents' income counts as well.

Sometimes a college will make an exception to this requirement, usually for a student it wants to recruit, and eligibility for federal Pell grants may be based on the income of the custodial parent only.

FAMILY HELP

In figuring the aid you're eligible for, colleges don't count what extended family or friends may contribute. But if your child's grandparents create a trust to pay for college, the Internal Revenue Service considers the income on the trust as income to you as a parent—since education is your responsibility.

However, grandparents—or anyone else—can make a direct gift to the college your child attends to offset the cost of tuition. That's not considered income to you, or a gift to your child.

WHAT IF YOU'RE THE STUDENT?

If the tuition you're concerned about is your own, most of the same rules apply. Your income will still determine the kind of aid you qualify for, but you may catch some breaks.

If you're older than 24, your parents' income doesn't count in figuring how much you can afford. That's true even if you live at home.

You also qualify for all the same federal grants and loans that a dependent student does. And if you're going back to school because you've lost your job or your marriage has dissolved, you may be eligible for a Pell grant even if you don't strictly meet the financial guidelines.

If you're planning a specific career, like teaching or certain kinds of medical work, or you're willing to commit yourself to a period of public service, you can sometimes get better loan terms.

Graduate schools often provide fellowships or other financial incentives for choosing their program. While you might owe taxes on money you get for teaching or other degree-related jobs, the institution will often help you find enough money to complete your degree.

10 THINGS TO KNOW ABOUT FINANCIAL AID

1 Colleges with aid-blind admissions policies admit students regardless of their need for aid. Some guarantee enough aid to allow everyone admitted to attend.

2 Your income during the calendar year before your child applies for aid establishes your eligibility.

3 Colleges are responding to increasing demand for aid by providing more of it—for the first year. But students find they are having to pay a larger share in the next three years, unless the college agrees to lock in the initial aid level.

4 It rarely works to claim that your child supports herself, since most colleges won't consider her independent and therefore eligible for aid in her own right until she turns 24.

5 Some colleges are willing to negotiate their initial aid offer, and others will reconsider, if you ask.

6 If your child qualifies for federal student aid, the government pays the interest on loans while she is enrolled in school.

7 Most financial aid loans are made to students, not parents. It is your child's responsibility to repay them.

8 As a parent, you can apply for a government-backed PLUS loan, which has capped interest rates, but no cap on borrowing.

9 About 60% of college graduates borrow money to pay for their educations, according to student loan source Nellie Mae. Debt averages $10,000 to $15,000 per student.

10 Scholarships or grants to cover expenses other than tuition are considered taxable income.

#4

Strategies for Paying

Persistence comes in handy when you're looking for ways to meet college costs.

Don't despair if you haven't invested enough to pay for your child's college education. You may qualify for financial aid, and there are a number of other strategies for raising the money you'll need.

Several of these approaches, like taking a home equity loan, involve long-term commitments and a level of risk you'll have to consider carefully. But it pays to know about the choices you have, since one of them may just be the solution you're looking for.

TUITION BULLETINS

PREPAYMENT PLANS

One way that state legislatures are trying to alleviate the anxiety of paying college expenses—and get much-needed money into their state university budgets right now—is to create prepayment programs.

These programs let you pay your child's tuition now, at today's rates, and guarantee that your costs will be covered when the time comes to enroll, even if it's years away. What's more, the programs guarantee your child's admission to at least one of the institutions covered by the agreement.

About 400,000 families nationwide have jumped at this opportunity, more than half in Florida, which has one of the oldest plans. Six other states have programs in place, six more have passed legislation to get a plan started, and still more are exploring it.

Before you rush to sign up, though, be sure to consider the potential downside.

THE DOWNSIDE OF PREPAYMENT

- What if your child—for very good reasons—wants to go someplace else to college, or drops out after the first year? While most programs refund your investment, they don't pay interest on the money they've held.

- What if the IRS decides that you owe income tax on the difference between the price you paid and the actual price of tuition when your child enrolls? That possibility has been tested once in court and may be again.

- What if you need the money for some other legitimate expense? What you've paid is locked up, so you can't get at it.

If you've got the money to prepay, critics of these programs say, why not put it in growth mutual funds, which have paid, on average, about 10% a year. That more than offsets the savings offered by the prepayment plans—namely the 6%–8% growth in college costs.

PRIVATE PREPAYMENT PLAN

The prepayment idea was actually invented by the College Savings Bank of Princeton (NJ). You invest the required amount in a CollegeSure CD, and they guarantee that you'll have enough to pay tuition when your child is ready for college. It's more flexible than the state- or college-sponsored plans because you're not committing your child to a specific college or university system—and a guarantee is a guarantee.

Why would anyone hesitate? Well, you do need a lump sum to invest. And if you've got that much in hand, you can almost certainly earn more with a different kind of investment, a stock mutual fund, for example.

WHAT'S NOT SMART

One of the conflicts you may wrestle with is deciding whether to use the money you've invested for retirement to pay for your child's education. Most financial advisors think it's a bad idea because it may leave you short of income later on. What's more, any money you withdraw from a qualified retirement plan, IRA or annuity will be immediately reduced by a 10% penalty unless you've reached age 59½. Experts also urge you to avoid borrowing against eligible plans since you may find it difficult to repay the borrowed amounts.

EDUCATION IRAS

Education IRAs are specifically designed to accumulate money for college. You can open one in a child's name at any financial institution that offers Education IRAs, and put away up to $500 a year per child to grow tax-deferred. No tax will be due on the earnings if you use the money to pay qualified educational expenses.

There are some limitations, though. There's an income cap limiting who can contribute. You can't put money in both a state-sponsored prepayment plan and an Education IRA in the same year, and you can't claim certain tuition tax credits any year you use money from that IRA.

HOME EQUITY LOANS

Your biggest ace in the hole when it comes to paying for college may be the equity you've built up in your home (see pages 116–117). That's because you can borrow more cheaply with a **home equity loan** than with any personal loan, and the interest you pay may be tax-deductible in most circumstances, lowering the cost of the loan even more.

If you bought your home when your child was small, the original mortgage may be nearly paid off.

That makes it easier to arrange an equity loan. And writing a check to the lender every month won't come as such a financial shock since you've been making mortgage payments all along.

Home equity loans are not a perfect solution, though. First, the money has to be paid back, usually starting immediately. And, if for some reason you **default**, or fail to pay back your loan, you run the very real risk of losing your home.

QUICKER DEGREES

If you're looking for other ways to save money on college costs, you might consider accelerated programs:

- Some colleges offer credit for high school advanced placement courses. That could mean finishing a degree a semester or even two early.

- Some colleges offer three-year programs that move students through their required courses more quickly.

- Credits earned at local colleges during summer school may count toward graduation and can reduce the number of semesters required. But have your child get the approval of her college first, to be sure it will accept the transfer credits.

A BOND DEAL

Baccalaureate bonds are something else to keep an eye out for. They're special tax-exempt zero-coupon bonds, usually sold in small denominations, so you can build up a portfolio of them on your own investment schedule. Because they're sold to come due on a specific date, you can time them so you'll have cash on hand every

semester or every year. Some of them provide an extra bonus if you use the money to pay tuition at an in-state school. But if you sell these bonds before they mature, you stand a good chance of losing money, as well as depleting funds you'll need for college.

Investing for Retirement
Whether it's down the road or just around the corner, retirement planning is a must.

#1

Retiring may be the last thing you want to do. Or it may be the goal that keeps you going. Whether or not you're planning *on* it, you should be planning *for* it. The reason is simple: you're going to need the money.

Unlike mortgages and educational expenses, which eventually get paid off, retirement means a permanent change—and usually a reduction—in the income you'll have to live on for the rest of your life. So when you cash your last paycheck, you'll need a substantial source of other income ready to fill the void.

How much of your current income you'll need

Since the income you'll need to live comfortably in retirement depends on your personal life style, there's no fixed amount that applies to everyone. But most retirement experts recommend that you plan to replace at least 80% of your preretirement income with pensions, Social Security and investments.

Many financial advisors who work with women urge them to plan to replace all their preretirement earnings, adjusted for inflation.

Where you'll get it

SOCIAL SECURITY + PENSION

Women earn only 60%–80% of what men earn, so they receive less from these two standard resources according to U.S. Bureau of the Census.

ESPECIALLY FOR WOMEN
Lining up retirement income is especially critical for women, since two of the standard resources—pensions and Social Security—are linked to a lifetime of earned income. Since women earn, on average, 20% to 40% less than men, and often work fewer years, they can expect to have less from those sources when they retire. For example, there has typically been a gap of about $200 a month in the Social Security benefits paid to men and women based on their earnings.

What's more, since women as a group live longer than men, they need income over a longer period of time. For example, women make up a large proportion of the fastest growing segment of the population: people over 80. That means living for many years on retirement income.

TIME TO COLLECT
You have to start withdrawing money from most tax-deferred plans by the time you reach age 70½ or when you retire, whichever comes later. Otherwise you'll be faced with a penalty.

A FIRM LEG TO STAND ON
Retirement income is generally described as a three-legged stool—balancing on your pension, Social Security and investment income. It's not hard to see what happens if one or more of those legs is missing or gets gnawed away. The remaining legs have to carry a greater share of the load.

That's why it is so critical to focus on investment strategy as a key part of your retirement planning. You have control over how much you invest, and what you invest in. As an added incentive to build your investments, you can put money in special tax-deferred retirement accounts that let you postpone taxes on your earnings until you start to take the money out—usually after you retire or by age 70½. That means you can buy and sell the investments in those accounts, reinvesting your interest and dividends to accumulate a substantial nest egg, without having to worry about paying tax on your gains each year.

TARGETED INVESTMENTS

There are three primary ways to invest for retirement. Each is taxed differently, which affects how much you'll end up with over time.

QUALIFIED RETIREMENT SAVINGS PLANS

Qualified retirement savings plans are almost always the best way to invest for the long term. Neither the amount you contribute, nor what you earn from the plan are taxed until you start taking the money out. Some qualified plans, like 401(k)s and 403(b)s, are sponsored by employers. There are also some plans you can use if you run your own business, like Keoghs, SEP-IRAs, or SIMPLES. Often, the contribution you make to these plans reduces your taxable salary or entitles you to a tax deduction—another immediate savings.

As an added bonus, when you start withdrawing after you retire, you may find you're paying tax at a lower rate than you would have paid when you put the money in. (You can't count on that, though, since there's no way to predict tax rates even a few years ahead.)

While qualified retirement plans are often called the best retirement investment you can make, they do have some limitations:

- There's a cap on the amount you can invest through the plans each year

- You usually can't use the money before you reach age 59½ without having to pay a 10% penalty on amounts you withdraw

+ INVESTMENTS

Investments produce the same results whether they're owned by men or women.

NON-QUALIFIED RETIREMENT PLANS

Non-qualified retirement plans, including annuities, also let your money grow tax-deferred. But because you invest money on which you've already paid tax, you'll have less to put into the account.

Some non-qualified plans have contribution limits and others don't, but all of them require you to pay a penalty on withdrawals before age 59½ in most circumstances.

REGULAR INVESTING

Regular investing is also a way to plan for retirement, since your long-term investments that aren't earmarked for other purposes continue to grow until you retire. Mutual funds you buy now, for example, can be a valuable source of retirement income, whether you need the money ten years from now—or 40.

One advantage of regular investing over a tax-deferred plan is that any increases in value are taxed at the lower, long-term **capital gains rate** if you've owned the investment at least a year before you sell. In contrast, money you withdraw from qualified and non-qualified retirement plans is taxed as regular income. Also, there's no limit on the amount you can invest and no restriction on when you can withdraw the money you've earned.

The downside of regular investments is that you've already paid tax on the money you invest, and you pay taxes every year on what the investment pays in interest or dividends—a big bite any way you look at it.

The Tax-Deferred Advantage

Not only will you accumulate more money over time, but you can often reduce your tax bill along the way.

Tax-deferred retirement plans let you postpone paying taxes on your earnings, giving you a jump-start on building your assets.

Instead of having to pay federal, state and sometimes local taxes on your earnings every year, your investment **compounds** untaxed. That means your earnings are added to your original investment to form a new investment base. As the base gets larger, it grows faster. In addition, each year you earn income, you can contribute more money to the plan, so the base amount continues to grow.

CONTRIBUTION LIMITS

Even if you could afford it, you can't stash every dollar you earn in a qualified retirement plan. IRAs, employer-sponsored plans and plans you set up yourself all have annual government-imposed limits.

TAX-DEFERRED INVESTING

Tax-deferred	$2,000
	INVESTMENT
Taxable	$2,000

There are limits, too, on some non-qualified plans, including the extra amounts you can contribute to an employer sponsored plan each year. There is one exception: there's no cap on the amount you can invest in fixed or variable annuities (see pages 138–139).

THE SALARY REDUCTION BONUS

If you participate in a salary reduction plan like a 401(k), or a plan you set up if you're self-employed, you can contribute part of your salary to a tax-deferred investment plan. You have an added advantage: the money you contribute reduces your salary, so it lowers your current income tax.

For example, if you earned $80,000 and contributed $8,000, the wages reported to the Internal Revenue Service would be $72,000. You would pay $2,480 less in tax on your own salary, so you would have that additional amount to invest elsewhere.

SALARY	$ 80,000	TAX ON $80,000:	$17,905[†]
− CONTRIBUTION	− $ 8,000		
= TAXABLE INCOME	$ 72,000	TAX ON $72,000:	$15,425[†]

[†]Based on single taxpayer, one exemption

In this example, the combined federal and state tax rate on the taxable investment is figured at 31%. Yours may be higher or lower, depending on your income, your filing status, and whether you pay state and local as well as federal income taxes.

PAY NO TAX UNTIL YOU WITHDRAW

HAVE MORE TO REINVEST

	$200	–	0	=	$2,200
+	ANNUAL 10% EARNINGS	–	TAX (IF ANY)	=	REINVESTMENT
+	$200	–	$62	=	$2,138

PAY TAX ON ALL EARNINGS ANNUALLY

HAVE LESS TO REINVEST

THREE WAYS TO INVEST

The bottom lines on your investment accounts emphasize the advantages of tax-deferred investing. Money invested in a qualified tax-deferred retirement plan like a 401(k) grows most, while money invested in a taxable account grows least, even when they're earning the same return.

Even after you pay the taxes due on your tax-deferred accounts as you withdraw, you'll still have more to show for your efforts.

Invest $2,000 a year in a qualified plan. Pay no tax on contributions or earnings until you withdraw.

Invest $1,360 after-tax dollars in a tax-deferred plan. Pay no tax on earnings until you withdraw.

Invest $1,360 after-tax dollars in taxable investments. Pay tax on earnings annually.

$244,692
ACCOUNT VALUE AFTER 30 YEARS*

$168,837
ACCOUNT VALUE AFTER 30 YEARS*

$105,846
ACCOUNT VALUE AFTER 30 YEARS*

Source: OppenheimerFunds

*Earnings at 8% before tax. Tax figured at 31% combined rate for single payer.

It Pays to Give at the Office

By reducing your paycheck a little, you can build your retirement savings a lot.

When you participate in a salary-reduction plan, you agree to have a percentage of your salary deducted from your paycheck and deposited in a retirement investment account. The amount that's deducted is considered **deferred income**, so you don't pay tax on it in the year you earn it.

Investing this way has a double advantage: your tax bill is smaller each year you contribute, and your retirement investments get a regular infusion of cash. Currently, fewer eligible women than men participate in employer-sponsored plans, something many financial advisors are concerned about.

WHAT'S A PRE-TAX DOLLAR?

Pre-tax dollars are what you earn before the amount you owe in federal, state and local taxes is subtracted. You invest pre-tax dollars in salary-reduction plans, but after-tax dollars in most other investments. Whatever your salary, you come out ahead when you take advantage of pre-tax investing.

IT'S YOUR CALL

Unlike Social Security taxes, which are automatically deducted from your salary, a salary-reduction plan lets you decide:

● **Whether to participate**

● **How much to contribute**

But sometimes having the choice may not be such a good thing—especially if you postpone signing up. The reality is, if you don't put in as much as you can each year, you may not have enough on hand when you're ready to retire.

WHAT YOUR CHOICES ARE

	THRIFT OR SAVINGS PLAN
Funding	Employer and employee
Contribution	Employer matches some or all of the amount an employee defers from pre-tax salary into the plan
Eligibility	Federal employees and employees of companies offering plans
Employee contribution limits	Up to $10,000 of earnings (in 1998)

MATCHING CONTRIBUTIONS

An important benefit of participating in a salary-reduction plan is that your employer may match part of your contribution. But if you don't contribute yourself, you miss out completely on the matching funds and the opportunity for retirement income.

The way that matching usually works is that for every dollar you contribute to the plan, your employer puts in something too—typically, half of what you contribute (but it might be less, or more). Often there's a cap, or upper limit, on how much of your contribution the employer will match. Typically, it's 6% of your salary.

YOUR CONTRIBUTION			EMPLOYER CONTRIBUTION			TOTAL
6%	of a $30,000 salary	$1,800	50%	of employee contribution	$900	$2,700
6%	of a $60,000 salary	$3,600	50%	of employee contribution	$1,800	$5,400
10%	of a $60,000 salary	$6,000	50%	of 6% of employee salary (cap applies)	$1,800	$7,800

WHEN YOU'RE ELIGIBLE

If your employer offers a qualified retirement plan, the eligibility rules have to be the same for every employee, from the boss on down. Usually, you can join the plan once you've been on the job full-time for a year, although some places let you begin contributing right away.

Some employers provide clearer information than others on what's available, or may have somebody on staff who can explain the alternatives to you. If you aren't sure what kind of plan is available, do some investigating. Even if you haven't given retirement planning much thought before, salary-reduction plans provide too many benefits to pass up. And some of them will even let you make up for missed time.

Your choice in tax-deferred salary-reduction plans depends on where you work. That's because specific plans have been authorized for different types of employers by different sections of the Internal Revenue Code.

401(k) PLAN	403(b) PLAN	SECTION 457 PLAN	SIMPLE PLAN
Employee and employer	Employee and employer	Employee	Employer and Employee
Employee contributes pre-tax salary to the plan; employer often contributes an additional amount	Employee contributes pre-tax salary into the plan; employers may match part of the amount	Employee contributes pre-tax salary to the plan	Employee contributes pre-tax salary; employer must contribute based on one of two formulas
All employees of businesses that sponsor plans	Restricted to employees of non-profit, tax-exempt organizations	Restricted to state and municipal workers	Available to companies with 100 or fewer employees
Up to $10,000 of earnings (in 1998)	Up to $10,000 of earnings (in 1998)	Up to $8,000 of earnings (in 1998)	Up to $6,000 of earnings

You're in the Driver's Seat

When you're making decisions, you can choose the route that's best for you.

Saying "yes" to a salary-reduction plan is a sound choice. But it moves you straight to the next set of decisions: what are your investment alternatives and which ones should you choose?

INVESTING THE MONEY

Salary-reduction plans are **self-directed**. You must choose how to invest your contribution, usually from a minimum of three to seven alternatives that your employer offers. The list generally includes equity, fixed income and money-market fund investments.

At least once a year, and sometimes more often, you can shift the money in your account from one investment to another. For example, you may want to transfer a part of a fixed income account into a fund that invests in stocks. Or you may want to put some of the money you've allocated to stocks into an international fund.

When you transfer money between annuity accounts, you don't owe income tax on your gains, although you may be charged a fee for moving money out of certain fixed-income accounts (see page 139).

MAKING IT WORK

If you decide to participate in a salary-reduction retirement plan, experts suggest two ways to make the most of it:

● **Contribute as much as you can every year that you're eligible**

● **Put your contributions into investments that you expect will increase the most in value over the long term**

SMOOTHING THE RIDE

There are two ways to strengthen performance in a salary reduction plan:

● **Monitor the performance of your plan's mutual funds against other funds with similar investment objectives.**
    To improve your investment's potential for long-term performance, you could request an expanded list of investment options, especially in stock mutual funds.

One thing working in your favor: executives have the same choices and pay the same fees as other employees, so there may be high-level support for changes.

● Check to see how much you're paying in management fees. Company pension funds typically pay .5% of their assets in fees, while the average 401(k) participant pays 1.4%.
    To reduce the fee, you and other employees may be able to persuade your employer to negotiate a group, rather than individual, fee structure. Since 401(k) accounts are a huge percentage of a mutual fund company's total investments, a fund might be willing to take a smaller fee to keep a client happy.

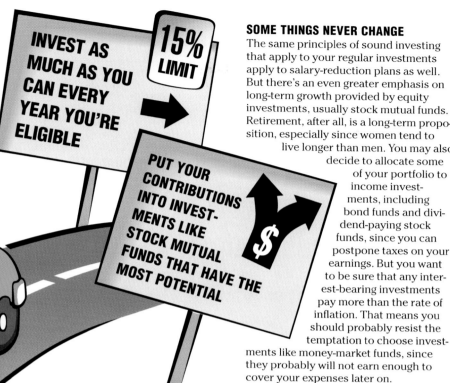

INVEST AS MUCH AS YOU CAN EVERY YEAR YOU'RE ELIGIBLE

15% LIMIT

PUT YOUR CONTRIBUTIONS INTO INVESTMENTS LIKE STOCK MUTUAL FUNDS THAT HAVE THE MOST POTENTIAL

SOME THINGS NEVER CHANGE

The same principles of sound investing that apply to your regular investments apply to salary-reduction plans as well. But there's an even greater emphasis on long-term growth provided by equity investments, usually stock mutual funds. Retirement, after all, is a long-term proposition, especially since women tend to live longer than men. You may also decide to allocate some of your portfolio to income investments, including bond funds and dividend-paying stock funds, since you can postpone taxes on your earnings. But you want to be sure that any interest-bearing investments pay more than the rate of inflation. That means you should probably resist the temptation to choose investments like money-market funds, since they probably will not earn enough to cover your expenses later on.

BY BEING TOO SAFE YOU RISK SORRY RESULTS

When you're choosing the investments for your retirement plans, you should consider those with greater growth potential. Although you'll benefit from compounding no matter which investments you choose, those with higher annual returns will grow more quickly than those with lower returns. For example, a 25-year investment yielding 10% produces a nest egg almost 80% larger than an investment yielding 4%.

25-year growth of $25,000

			$120,599
		$73,402	
	$44,650		
$27,138			
4%	6%	8%	10%

Source: OppenheimerFunds

A LIFELONG COMPANION

If you change jobs frequently—and women tend to move at least as often as men—there's a good chance you'll be eligible for less retirement income than if you'd stayed put. But if you're contributing to a salary reduction plan, you can beat the odds.

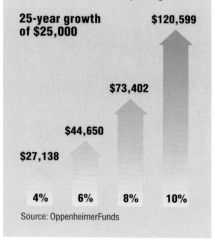

401(k)

That's because **contributory plans** are portable. When you change jobs, you can often transfer your investments to your new employer's plan, or you can move your accumulated assets into a rollover IRA account, where they'll continue to grow tax-deferred. (Be careful, though. You must have these transfers made directly to the new account to avoid potential tax problems. Check with your tax advisor or other expert before you act.)

Also, with a contributory plan, the money you put in is yours right from the start. You don't have to wait to be **vested**, which means holding a job long enough to be guaranteed a pension. By one estimate, many women abandon potential retirement earnings each year by leaving a job before they're vested.

IRAs

An IRA can be your first line of defense in protecting your future.

No retirement plan? You're not alone. While 75% of American women work, only about half of them are currently covered by a pension plan. But an **Individual Retirement Account (IRA)**, or personal retirement savings plan, is available to anyone who earns income or is married to someone who does.

With an IRA you can invest up to $2,000 each year and defer income taxes on your earnings, which are reinvested. You have the potential for faster growth than if you were paying taxes on an account earning the same rate of return. And depending on your income, you may qualify for the additional tax advantages of being able to lower your current taxes by deducting your contribution or selecting a Roth IRA with its promise of eventual tax-free income.

GOOD REASONS TO OPEN AN IRA

- **Have a personal savings plan**

- **Benefit from tax-deferred earnings**

- **Build your retirement account**

- **Choose among a variety of investments**

A TAX BREAK FOR TRADITIONAL IRAs

If you meet either one of the qualifying tests, you can deduct your traditional IRA contribution on your income tax return.

TEST #1
LEVEL OF INCOME

You can deduct your IRA contribution if your income is less than the annual ceiling. In 1998, you can take the full $2,000 if your income is less than $30,000 and you're single, or your joint income is less than $50,000 if you're married. For each additional $1,000 in income, you can deduct $200 less, until the deduction is phased out entirely at $40,000 (single) and $60,000 (married). Those amounts will increase gradually through 2007.

**A T A X
B R E A K
T O   B O O T**

Your IRA contribution reduces your taxable income—and therefore your taxes—if you meet one of the two qualifying tests.

TEST #2
RETIREMENT PLAN COVERAGE

If there isn't a pension or salary-reduction plan available where you work, you can deduct your contribution and reduce your taxes. This deduction applies whether you are single or married. Even if your husband is part of a pension plan or is contributing to a salary-reduction plan, it doesn't affect your eligibility. But there is an income cap. However, contributions to Roth IRAs are never deductible.

JUST SAY IT'S SO

You can establish an Individual Retirement Account with a bank, brokerage firm, or mutual fund company, or an Individual Retirement Annuity with an insurance company. When you fill out the paperwork and deposit your money, the IRA exists. It's as simple as that.

The institution acts as custodian or trustee and invests the money as you direct in stocks, bonds, mutual funds, CDs—the same kinds of investments that are available outside an IRA except art, jewelry, real estate and collectibles.

You usually pay an annual fee—$10 to $50—plus whatever other charges there may be for maintaining the account. Some custodians waive fees, though, if your account is large enough. That can be a persuasive argument for consolidating your IRA investments.

DON'T STOP NOW

To get tax-deferred growth, you agree that if you withdraw from your account before you reach age 59½, you'll owe a 10% penalty plus the tax that's due on the withdrawal amount, in most cases. But you can still put money into your IRA after you reach age 59½, when you could start taking it out. The investment account continues to grow tax-deferred, and you can tap it anytime you need the money without paying the early withdrawal penalty. You must begin taking money out of your traditional IRA in the year after you turn 70½, and must withdraw at least the required amount. The way you figure that amount is spelled out in IRS Publication 590. You can work with your financial or tax advisor to be sure you get it right.

HOW NOT TO DO IT

Sometimes it's easier to decide how to make an investment decision—in this case, where to put your IRA money—by being clear on what you should *not* do. Here is what many financial experts warn against:

⊘ Don't buy tax-free investments, like municipal bonds or municipal bond funds, for a traditional IRA because all earnings are ultimately taxable.

⊘ Don't invest in low-interest savings and money-market accounts, because you won't earn enough to offset inflation.

⊘ Don't get locked into an investment that isn't living up to expectations. You can move IRA money easily from one investment to another without owing tax on earnings.

⊘ Don't open a different IRA account every year. You'll pay more in fees, and you'll have more records to keep track of.

⊘ Don't lose your tax records of non-deductible IRA investments. If you can't prove the tax was paid, you may pay tax twice on the same money.

ROTH OR TRADITIONAL?

Because there are choices in IRAs, between the traditional type and the newer Roth IRA, you need to know how they compare to select between them.

The appeal of the Roth is that you get the added benefit of tax-free income on your tax-deferred earnings when you take money out, provided you're older than 59½ and your account has been open at least five years. That adds up to more money in your pocket.

But to be eligible to contribute the full $2,000 to a Roth, your income must be less than $95,000 (with partial contributions phased out at $110,000) if you're single, and your joint income less than $150,000 (phased out at $160,000) if you're married. The contributions are never deductible.

In contrast, everyone qualifies for a traditional IRA, and, as the tests opposite show, in some cases you may be eligible to deduct your contribution, reducing current tax.

Many experts advise choosing a Roth if you qualify, and add that it may pay to transfer your existing IRA to a Roth. But they all agree that before you make a decision it's smart to talk to your own advisor or someone at the bank, mutual fund company or brokerage firm where you have your existing account or plan to open a new one.

EARLY WITHDRAWALS

Though IRAs are intended as long-term retirement investments, you may be able to withdraw your accumulated assets without the 10% federal tax penalty in some very specific situations.

For example, you can use IRA money to pay college tuition, spend up to $10,000 of it to buy a first home for yourself or someone else, or use it for medical expenses. While you will usually owe the income tax that applies to the withdrawal amounts, you won't owe the extra 10%.

The best approach, if you need your IRA money for one of these purposes, is to confirm that your plans meet the tax requirements before taking out the money.

More Tax-Deferred Alternatives

You can cultivate the fertile soil of tax-deferred investing in lots of different ways.

The rewards of tax-deferred investing—faster growth and the potential for reduced taxes—are ideal reasons to seize every opportunity to salt away money for retirement. And you don't have to work for someone else to take advantage of tax-deferral. You can set up your own plan if you're self-employed. You can inherit tax-deferred investments from your husband. Or you can invest using a spousal IRA.

Spousal IRAs

If you don't have earned income, you can't contribute to a salary-reduction plan. But, your husband can contribute to a spousal IRA, setting aside a total of $4,000 a year divided into two equal accounts. For example, he could put $2,000 in his own account and $2,000 in yours. Or he could put $2,000 in yours, but nothing in his own. The only restriction is that the cap for any one account is $2,000.

Your spousal IRA grows tax-deferred, in your name. And it won't keep you from contributing to an IRA someday yourself, if you earn income. You can invest the money as you see fit, eventually withdraw it and spend it as you wish. A spousal IRA is an ideal way for women who stay at home with their children to get a head start on building a retirement fund.

BOTH WORKING

 +  =

$4,000
Maximum contribution $2,000 each

ONE WORKING

 +  =

$4,000
Maximum contribution, $2,000 each after 1996 legislation

Keoghs and SEPs

There are lots of good reasons to work for yourself, most of them unrelated to retirement investing. But self-employment does give you the chance to establish a tax-deferred, tax-deductible plan that lets you invest for the future at the same time as you're earning a living.

Like other qualified retirement plans, Simplified Employee Pensions (SEPs) and Keoghs enjoy the benefits of tax-deferral, both on the investment amount and the annual earnings. As with other plans, you can put the money to work in a broad range of investments, all selected by you.

What gives Keoghs and SEPs their added appeal is their higher contribution limit—up to 15% of earnings, with a cap of $22,500, for SEPs and some Keoghs, and up to 25% of earnings, with a cap of $30,000, for other Keoghs.

But since there are tax implications to setting up these plans, you should always consult your accountant or other tax advisor. That will save you headaches, and probably money.

HOW THEY WORK

While both Keoghs and SEPs are qualified retirement plans that limit access to your funds until age 59½ and require you to start withdrawing when you reach age 70½ or retire, there are some important differences between them, as the chart on the following page shows.

Rollovers

If you have money in an employer's qualified retirement plan or your own Keogh plan, you can usually transfer it to a Rollover IRA if:

- **You leave your job or retire**

- **Your husband dies and you get a payout from his employer**

- **You receive payment from an eligible plan that has ended**

- **You get money from your ex-husband's qualified plan as part of a divorce settlement**

Rolling over your retirement funds into an IRA—rather than spending them or using them to cover anything short of an outright emergency—is essential if you want to keep up the investment momentum you've established. What's more, you may be able to roll the money back into a new employer's retirement plan provided the money was kept in a separate account.

IRA TO IRA

Moving money from one IRA directly to another—for example, from a bank to a mutual fund—is a tax-free transaction, even if you transfer an account that has earned thousands of dollars in dividends and interest.

However, you have to put the entire withdrawal into the new IRA within 60 days after taking it out of the old one. If you miss the cut-off, you'll owe taxes and, potentially, a penalty. And, remember, you can roll over an IRA only once a year.

INTO A ROTH?

If your annual income is less than $100,000, you qualify to roll over your existing IRAs into a tax-free Roth IRA. In the year you transfer, you will have to pay tax on your accumulated earnings and on any contributions you deducted, but there'll be no tax when you eventually withdraw if you're over 59½ and the account has been open five years. It can be a smart move, but you ought to consult a financial expert before you decide.

KEEPING AHEAD OF THE TAXMAN

If you roll over retirement money directly to the custodian or trustee of your Rollover IRA, it's a tax-free transaction, and the entire amount goes on growing tax-deferred. But if the payout goes to you first, 20% is automatically withheld even if you deposit the check immediately in the rollover account.

You'll eventually get the 20% back—provided you've deposited the entire amount of the payout within 60 days. But you'll have to wait for the refund until you've filed your income tax return.

The real rub is coming up with the missing 20% in order to make the full deposit. If you don't, the IRS treats that amount as a withdrawal and you'll owe tax (and maybe penalty on it).

The solution: always do a direct rollover.

SAVE 20% NOW

ADVANTAGES

KEOGHS

- Offer several ways to structure a plan
- May let you shelter more money than some other plans
- Allow employers to set criteria for employees to qualify for participation

SEPS

- Simpler and cheaper to set up
- Easier to administer, both internally and for the IRS
- Don't commit you to annual contributions

LIMITATIONS

- Can commit you to contributions even in poor years
- Expensive to set up and administer
- Complex tax-reporting requirements

- Contribution amount limited to 15%
- Employers must cover all employees, but may set eligibility requirements based on years of service

Deferred Annuities

Annuities are tax-deferred savings plans that may or may not be right for you.

If you're putting as much as you can into your salary-reduction plan, how else can you build your retirement investments? One possibility is fixed or variable annuities, which also offer tax-deferred growth along with insurance that provides the option of lifetime income and a guaranteed death benefit for your beneficiaries.

SPELLING IT OUT

When you buy an annuity as a **non-qualified retirement plan**, the earnings on your contribution—known as the inside buildup—accumulate tax-deferred. But you pay taxes on the investment amount before you put it into the annuity, just as you do with a nondeductible IRA.

Annuity CONTRACT

1. I agree to invest my money now.

2. You'll pay me back, plus earnings, when the annuity matures.

☐ **FIXED ANNUITY**

A **fixed annuity** guarantees you'll earn at least a specific rate of interest over the life of the annuity, although what you actually earn in any given period may fluctuate in response to changes in the general interest rate or some other benchmark. These annuities are insurance company products, though they're sold by financial advisors and bank reps as well as insurance agents.

May I. Durell

☐ **VARIABLE ANNUITY**

A **variable annuity** lets you select various mutual fund investment portfolios, also called subaccounts, from a specific list of choices. What you earn depends on how well the subaccounts you've selected perform. Variable annuities are insurance company products that are sold through a variety of licensed financial advisors.

ANOTHER VARIATION ON THE THEME

There's one more way to put your money in an annuity: many qualified retirement plans, 403(b)s, for example, offer annuities as one of the investment choices for salary-reduction plans. The overall advantages and disadvantages of investing in annuities apply here as well. Annuity advocates argue that receiving a guaranteed stream of income after you retire is exactly the reason you're investing your money now.

Critics of annuities ask why you should face the possibility of paying a penalty if you want to switch out of an annuity into another investment. They also point out that since your retirement plan is already tax-deferred, there's little additional advantage in choosing an annuity.

ANNUITIES—PROS AND CONS

You may be asking yourself why, if annuities seem to have so many advantages, they are controversial. Here's a summary of their strengths and their weaknesses:

THE GOOD

- Your investment grows tax-deferred and a portion of your income may be tax-free
- Variable annuities make your investment decisions easier by narrowing your choices to a pre-selected group of investment portfolios
- Variable annuities offer potential for strong growth and inflation protection
- No-load variable annuities are available
- There are generally no caps on the amount you can invest each year
- You frequently have your choice of payout—lump sum or lifetime income
- Many products allow immediate access to earnings

THE QUESTIONABLE

- If you select an annuity payout, there may be gender bias. As a woman, you'll generally pay a higher premium or get a smaller payout than a man of the same age because, statistically, you'll live longer
- Annual fees on variable annuities may be higher than the fees on comparable mutual funds, which means you must earn more to make out as well
- Earnings payouts are taxed as ordinary income, not as capital gains. That means you'll pay a higher tax rate than if you invested in products that benefit from capital gains treatment
- Most annuities have surrender fees—typically 7% or more of the amount you invest—if you decide to end the contract during the surrender-charge period
- With fixed annuities, the safety of your investment depends on the financial strength of the insurance company selling you the annuity

IF NOT AN ANNUITY, THEN WHAT?

If you're looking for additional ways to invest for retirement, here are some things you may want to consider:

- Putting money into mutual funds and stocks that emphasize growth, which minimizes current taxes. You can set up a regular payout schedule when you start collecting. Plus, these investments are taxed as capital gains.
- Staggering your bond investments so that they mature in different years. This will ensure a regular flow of income and keep your reinvestment choices flexible
- Buying municipal bonds and municipal bond funds—the income is generally tax-exempt
- Buying U.S. Savings Bonds

INVESTMENT VS. PENSION PAYOUT

Don't confuse a deferred annuity with a **pension annuity**. A pension annuity, sometimes called a life-stream payment, is the standard method of collecting the retirement income your employer pays you. It means getting a check each month for the remainder of your life.

If you're eligible for a pension, taking it as an annuity makes lots of sense. By law, employers must use the same life expectancy table for women as for men in calculating the amount of your monthly payment. But, as a woman, you're likely to live longer—and so collect more—than a man the same age.

Coping with the Unexpected

You have to be prepared to deal with the things you can't prevent.

However carefully you plan your financial security, there are events that can throw your life into turmoil. That's why it's important, even if it's painful, to think about the financial consequences of divorce or widowhood, and the need for health care as you grow older. While there's no foolproof way to predict or prevent future events, there are things you can do now to make your economic position more secure—whatever the future brings.

WHY IT MATTERS

Whether or not you are primarily responsible for handling your financial affairs now, the chances are overwhelming that you will be in the future. That's true in large part because the majority of widowed women, and many divorced women, do not remarry.

If you put off learning about financial matters until you are faced with a crisis, you're certain to regret it. And there's no point in letting yourself feel vulnerable when you can do something about it. Probably the best approach is to develop a working relationship with your husband or partner to make investing and other financial decisions a cooperative effort.

THE FIRST STEP

As a start, you need to know where you stand financially. If your family finances are clearly organized, your job will be much easier. But if they're not organized, the first thing you have to do is get your records in order. You can start by reviewing your joint tax returns, checkbook registers and charge card records. You can also get in touch with the benefits or personnel officer at your job, and at your husband's job, to check on pension and other retirement plans and on health insurance.

In a worst-case scenario, where you can't find the information you need, there are ways to retrieve computer files and get hold of other records. You'll probably want to consult your lawyer about the best way to proceed.

GETTING THE FINANCIAL FACTS

When you put together your financial profile, here's some of what you'll want to know:

- How much money are you living on and where does it come from?

- What investments do you have, and where are they held or recorded?

- Which of your investments could you turn into cash easily if you needed money?

- What pension and other retirement plans exist and who administers them?

- What are your family's life and health insurance arrangements?

- How much do you owe and to whom?

- Does your husband have a will? Do you? Where are they?

GETTING ADVICE

One thing you'll need in the event of divorce or widowhood, and at other times of financial change, is professional advice. In particular, you may want an advisor who is experienced in working with people whose situations are similar to your own. As you'll discover—hopefully before it happens to you—many of the decisions you make at the time of divorce or widowhood, such as those concerning alimony or pension payout, cannot be changed even if you later realize that you've made a bad decision. Legal and financial help is important, too, when you're dividing property and settling estates, since it can be easy to overlook critical details.

You may prefer to go on working with an advisor that you and your husband used together, or you might prefer someone you choose on your own. In either case, you'll find that the advice of someone you trust will make the decision-making process much less traumatic.

GIVE YOURSELF CREDIT

If you're wondering whether it makes sense to have a credit card in your own name, the answer is probably yes. That way, there's no question about access to credit in the aftermath of divorce or widowhood. Even if your initial credit line is relatively small, card issuers are happy to increase the amount you can borrow provided you charge regularly and pay on time.

In case of divorce, you will certainly need your own credit account since all joint arrangements are ended, either at the time of official separation or when the divorce is final. As a widow, you'll be able to go on using the cards you and your husband have had together. But in the long run, you'll probably need your own.

If you have a regular job and a credit history, it should be relatively easy to get a card. If you don't work but you've been using credit cards held in both your names, you have also established a credit history. That's probably the most important requirement for having a credit card application approved.

FAMILY RECORDS

You should have detailed and up-to-date records that describe your family assets. It's usually best if you and your husband gather the information together, before you need it, and straighten out things you're not clear about. Here's a list of items to include:

 Checking and savings accounts

 Stock and bond certificates in a safe deposit box or other secure place

 Investment accounts with a brokerage, bank, mutual fund or other financial institution

 Pension and other retirement plans administered by current or past employers

 Insurance policies and wills

 Titles to real estate, cars and other holdings

 Business documents and partnership agreements

 Appraisal documents for collections

 Records of outstanding loans

 Tax records

Divorce: Financial Self-Defense

You can protect what you have by developing your own financial expertise.

The end of a marriage often means major financial changes. The unfortunate reality is that a divorced woman usually ends up losing out economically, especially if she has been dependent on her husband's income. Since nearly half of all marriages end in divorce, many women have cause for concern.

However, you can protect yourself if you're prepared to handle day-to-day finances and make investment decisions on your own. The more confident you are about your financial skills, the more prepared you'll be.

If you've developed your financial skills, a divorce won't mean you'll find yourself on the defensive

WHAT'S AT STAKE

In legal terms, divorce is about dividing up property and resolving issues of child custody and support. If you have few assets and no children, there may be no controversy. Otherwise, you may have to be prepared for a struggle. Although about 90% of all divorces are settled out of court, the most contentious ones can take a long time to resolve.

The more you know about what assets there are and how and where they are held, the more accurate a picture you'll have of what to ask for in the settlement. Being able to demonstrate the amount you've contributed financially to the marriage, and to building the assets, may also give you more leverage.

One of the most difficult issues is the question of equitable distribution of marital property, the standard in most states. *Equitable* does not mean *equal*. It is more apt to mean a two-thirds/one third split, with the more affluent partner getting the larger share.

In the nine **community property** states (Arizona, California, Idaho, Louisiana, Nevada, New Mexico, Texas, Washington and Wisconsin), marital property is defined as anything earned or owned jointly during the marriage. It is divided equally, in most cases.

Future income is not property, and is not subject to division, equitable or otherwise. That often explains the disparity between men's and women's financial situations following a divorce: if women earn less, they are more likely to have less in the long run.

AVOIDING KNOCKOUT PUNCHES

Since divorce can raise legal and financial questions you haven't faced before, it's important to get professional advice before you make any major decisions. Unless you have a good grasp of your finances to share with your advisor, you may run into added expenses and potential delays in dissolving the marriage.

QUESTIONS OF DEBT

If your marriage has come apart over financial issues, a divorce may not resolve the problems. That's because any debts either of you incurred while you were married, and any joint agreements you signed, will probably be considered your responsibility if your former husband does not pay them. If you refuse to pay, or can't afford to, your personal credit history could be affected.

Creditors might also try to collect from you on debts your husband runs up during the time you're legally separated. Escaping these demands may be more difficult than you would think. One of the issues that will affect the outcome is how your state defines legal separation.

One of you could agree to pay off debt in exchange for a larger share of the assets. You want to be aware, though, that if your former husband declares bankruptcy after the divorce, an IOU he has given you may be worthless.

You are also responsible to the IRS for any unpaid taxes that are due on joint returns you've signed, even if you weren't involved in figuring the tax or filling out the forms. But you should not be held responsible for taxes on income your former husband might have concealed from you—and from the IRS.

LOCAL CONTROL

Divorces are regulated by state laws, and court settlements generally reflect local custom rather than any uniform state or national standard. That means it may be hard to know how the financial details of a contested case will turn out. The only way to anticipate what's likely to happen is to find out the pattern local judges follow in dividing property and awarding custody. You should get advice from an experienced lawyer.

UNILATERAL ACTIONS

If you decide on your own to move out of the house, or take your children to live at any distance from their father or in a different state, it can have serious negative consequences, especially if your case ends up in court. Be sure you explore less dramatic moves and find out what the downside of moving away can be.

FACING THE REALITY

Whether you initiate the decision to end your marriage or have it imposed on you, there are some things experts suggest you consider to sidestep potential financial problems:

- Establish your own checking, savings and credit accounts as soon as divorce seems inevitable. If your existing accounts are joint, you can ask your lawyer's advice about withdrawing half the balance to open your own account. Technically, you, or your husband, can take out every penny. But if you do, you might face a court order to repay it, or prejudice your legal case.

- If you are able to work amicably, consider an escrow account or joint account requiring both signatures to pay family expenses in the time between separation and divorce.

- Make a new will and designate a new beneficiary for insurance policies, pension and retirement plans, and any other assets passed directly to a beneficiary. Existing wills are often voided when a divorce is final.

- Cancel joint-equity lines of credit and freeze joint brokerage accounts. Otherwise, you might end up with more debt or fewer investments than you expected. You can call first, and send a follow-up letter. If you ask that a notation be made on the account's computer file, you may be able to prevent unauthorized trades.

- Ask your lawyer about changing real property that you own as joint tenants to tenants in common (see page 31), so you can designate your heir(s) if you die before the divorce is final. In some states you can do this individually, by filing a record of the deed change where the original deed is registered. In other states, you must both agree to the change, so be sure to check.

JOINT CUSTODY

Agreeing on custody of your children may be one of your most difficult decisions. In recent years, shared custody has provided the solution for some families. But you may find that shared, or joint, custody means smaller child-support payments. If you're dividing costs equitably, that can be fine. But if you're footing the bills for most expenses, receiving less money can be a real problem. One solution may be to try to resolve each parent's financial responsibilities in the divorce agreement.

Financial Settlements

As the dust settles, you can start building your future.

If you're confident about what you want, rational about why you want it and realistic about what you can reasonably expect to get, you can use your divorce settlement as the foundation for your future financial security. But if you don't have a clear plan for handling your share of the assets, what seems like a fair deal at the time can erode under your feet—or turn to quicksand.

Once the settlement is final, having a plan in place can also help you avoid potential problems, such as making risky investments, overextending your credit, or tapping into IRAs or other retirement funds to meet daily expenses.

YOURS, MINE AND OURS

Ownership determines division of property. Generally speaking, anything you owned in your own name before marriage, and continued to hold separately, is yours to keep, as is anything you inherited or received as a gift.

But money that you and your husband earned during the marriage, along with your investments and property, is divided at divorce. If you can agree on the division without going to court, you save money—sometimes astounding amounts.

In most cases, though, you'll probably benefit from the advice and assistance of an experienced divorce attorney, especially if there's a lot to divide.

DIVIDING RETIREMENT PLANS

In evaluating your marital assets, you may discover that substantial amounts of money are tied up in a pension or other retirement fund. If you both have plans, you may each agree to keep your own. But if you have no plan, or a small one, you can claim a share of your husband's.

To do that, a lawyer must draw up a Qualified Domestic Relations Order (QDRO) as part of the divorce settlement. That's a court order that instructs the administrator of his plan—*not* your soon-to-be-ex-husband—to divide the pension assets between you. To achieve the results you want, the order must be specific and accurate, so you should consult a specialist in the field.

Since the administrator has 18 months to rule on the validity of the QDRO, you can also ask that your share of the assets be set aside, so that they can't be withdrawn or borrowed. The way the pension will be paid out, and the other rights you may have—taking loans, for example—will depend on the plan. So be sure that you understand the provisions clearly.

THE ELEMENTS OF A FAIR DEAL

In agreeing to a divorce settlement, there are more important things than just getting it over with. Chief among them is considering the long-term implications of dividing assets.

Your lawyer or financial advisor can provide advice, but if you can provide the details, you'll owe less in fees. And the more you know about the assets and what they're worth, the better you'll understand how to divide them.

Obviously, each case is different, but there are several things you should always consider.

One is taxes. You owe no taxes when you get something as part of a divorce settlement. But if you later sell the property at a profit you can owe **capital gains taxes**. For example, if you sell stock or mutual fund shares to make a downpayment on a new home, you'll owe tax at your capital gains rate. The one exception is selling your home, since you can realize up to $250,000 in profit as a single person without owing any tax.

Another consideration is the quality and diversity of the investments that you receive. You

GETTING SOCIAL SECURITY

If you were married ten years or longer before your divorce, you're entitled to receive Social Security based on your ex-husband's earnings. He actually isn't involved—it's between you and the Social Security office—and his benefits aren't diminished. But it can be an important resource, especially if your own benefit would be smaller, or if you wouldn't qualify for Social Security on your own.

INSURANCE PROTECTION

If you or your children are dependent on income from your ex-husband, you'll probably want to make sure he has life insurance to replace that income if he dies or is disabled. There are various ways to pay so that you know the coverage is kept up to date. One is for you to be the owner as well as the beneficiary of the policy. But however you handle it, insurance is an important detail to include in your settlement.

THE ALIMONY QUESTION

Whether or not you receive income from your ex-husband after your divorce depends on a number of factors, especially the length of your marriage, your financial and life style situations, your ability to support yourself and sometimes the tax implications. It rarely matters who initiates the divorce, or whether or not blame can be attached to either of you for the breakup.

If you've had a long marriage, often defined as one lasting more than 15 years, you may be more likely to receive alimony. The tendency, however, in most states is to limit the number of years alimony has to be paid, under the assumption that women will be prepared to support themselves after that time. Of course, in some circumstances, you could be the one paying alimony.

You should also be aware that while there are increasingly strong mechanisms in place to require divorced and separated parents—usually but not always the fathers—to pay child support regularly, it can be more difficult to collect alimony from a former husband if he is unwilling to pay it.

In recent years, there has been a movement to set statewide standards for child support as a percentage of income and a reflection of existing life style. The same has not been true for alimony, which can vary enormously both within a particular state and from state to state.

If you feel strongly that you would rather terminate all ties to—and dependence on—your former husband, you may prefer a one-time payment that you can invest and manage as you choose.

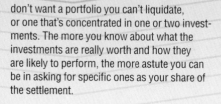

don't want a portfolio you can't liquidate, or one that's concentrated in one or two investments. The more you know about what the investments are really worth and how they are likely to perform, the more astute you can be in asking for specific ones as your share of the settlement.

Widowhood

Widowhood means starting again, with added responsibility for your financial affairs.

Though it's not a welcome thought, the fact is that women are likely to outlive their husbands. In fact, there are five times as many widows as widowers in the U.S. Widows live an average of 15 years after their husbands die, and are also much less likely to remarry than widowed men are, especially if they're over age 45.

As a woman, that means that you must be prepared to make financial decisions, whether or not you have done so during your marriage. They may be sweeping decisions involving large sums of money, or careful ones designed to stretch limited dollars as far as they will go. In either case, you can go about it more confidently if you're ready for the task.

PENSION PAYOUTS

If your husband has a pension from his employer that provides an **annuity**, or regular monthly payment after he retires, federal law requires that it's paid as a **joint and survivor annuity**, which spreads the pension payments over both your husband's lifetime and yours, so you go on receiving income after he dies.

If you agree in writing at the time he retires that the pension should be paid as a **single life annuity**, it will provide income during his lifetime only. Most experts advise you *not* to agree to this unless you have a good pension of your own, or there is a strong chance that your husband will survive you.

However, a joint and survivor annuity pays less each month than a single life, since it covers a potentially longer time period. If you should die suddenly, your husband would end up with a reduced amount for the remainder of his life.

But it's risky—probably too risky—to give up the lifetime income guaranteed by the joint and survivor annuity. What's more, if you live long enough, the total you receive could well surpass what a single life annuity would have paid. None of the alternatives that may be suggested to you, such as using some of your husband's payout to buy an annuity for you—sometimes called a pension maximization plan—will provide the same level of security as a joint and survivor annuity.

Your husband must also get your agreement before he can name anyone but you as the beneficiary of his 401(k). However, when he retires he can roll over the full amount into an IRA and name any beneficiary he likes.

GENDER MATTERS

If you're entitled to a pension, it will have the same provision making a joint and survivor annuity mandatory, unless your husband agrees to a different payout plan. Since most women survive their husbands, retirement experts generally advise you to choose a single life payout, providing of course that your husband agrees. It may not be an ideal choice in every case, especially if you're in frail health. But decisions about payouts, after all, are only calculated risks about the best way to insure the largest income stream for the longest period of time.

COLLECTING A PAYOUT

In choosing the way a pension or immediate annuity is paid, you have to balance the amount you'll receive each month against whether it will cover one lifetime or two. You can compare three alternatives in this hypothetical case which assumes a $50,000 annuity payment schedule.

Type of payout	Retiree's pay-out until death	Death of retiree	Surviving spouse's monthly payout
Single life	$4,167		Nothing
50% joint and survivor	$3,705		$1,853
100% joint and survivor	$3,335		$3,335

FINAL DETAILS

If your husband dies, you'll discover there are financial and legal issues that have to be resolved. In most cases, you can work with your financial advisor and lawyer to get them taken care of promptly. Among the things that you may have to be prepared to handle:

- Contacting Social Security to report his death and your status as a widow if he was collecting benefits

- Notifying his employer, IRA custodians and insurance agent, and requesting settlement payments

- Changing joint bank, mutual fund and brokerage accounts to your name

- Recording your ownership of real estate, cars and other property

- Paying his bills, including income taxes

YOUR RIGHTS AS A WIDOW

It's important to know what your legal rights are when it comes to inheritance. Since each state's laws are a little different, it's best to check with your lawyer or advisor. But in general, you're entitled to a percentage—usually 33% to 50%—of your husband's estate *whether or not* he leaves it to you in his will.

For example, if a married man left his entire estate to his brother and nothing to his wife, the courts would overturn his wishes, to the extent state law required.

By the same token, if your husband dies without a will, you may get only the percentage of his estate the law requires, even if it was his intention to leave you everything. That's why it's so important for you and your husband to have wills. Though many people avoid wills because they seem premonitions of doom, they are critical financial documents.

INHERITING JOINT PROPERTY

If you and your husband own property as joint tenants with rights of survivorship, all of the property—whether real estate, bank accounts, brokerage accounts or other holdings—becomes yours automatically at his death. All you need to do is transfer the title to your name.

But while ownership is not an issue, taxes may be, if you decide to sell the property. Here's how it works: the half that belonged to your husband is **stepped up**, or appraised at its current worth, in figuring the value of his estate. If you sold the property promptly, there would be no **capital gain** or increase in value over the stepped up appraisal, so there would be no capital gains tax. However, your half of the same property may be subject to capital gains. That's just one of the reasons you should discuss tax planning, both as a couple and as a widow, with your accountant or other financial advisor.

HANDLING LUMP-SUM PAYOUTS

If you're named as the beneficiary of your husband's 401(k), IRA or other retirement plan, that money is paid to you directly after his death. Many experts advise you to roll over any tax-deferred retirement plans or IRAs into an IRA in your own name. You can roll over the money without owing any tax until you begin withdrawing—an added advantage. You can also invest the money to meet your goals, following the strategies described in chapters five and six.

Managing on Your Own

As a widow, your investing pace might change, but the dual goals of growth and income endure.

The riskiest things you can do as a widow are to act quickly and to decide—or be persuaded—that you're not able to manage your own affairs. Taking your time doesn't mean delaying decisions indefinitely. Nor does it mean refusing to take advice. But it is essential to plan carefully as you move ahead.

In contrast, one of the smartest things you can do is take a hard look at the goals you have been pursuing and the investments you own. That assessment may mean you'll want to make some changes. Or you may be comfortable with things the way they are. There's no one solution that works well for everyone.

The kinds of investments that make good sense in other life situations— mutual funds, stocks and bonds—usually make good sense in widowhood. And having a strong financial plan in place is at least as important to you as a widow as it is at other times in your life.

But you also have to look carefully at some investments that are often suggested to widows. While they can seem like ideal solutions, they may not provide the growth and income you need for the rest of your life and you could be locked into your decision. Before you commit to anything, most experts suggest you get a second opinion from an independent financial advisor whose impartial advice can help you evaluate the pros and cons.

STOP AND CALMLY ASSESS YOUR SITUATION

USE CAUTION IN YOUR INVESTING

A WIDOW'S INVESTMENT GOALS

Your financial goals as a widow may focus first on having enough income to cover your living expenses. But there are really three basic goals to keep in mind:

- **Preservation of principal**
- **Income**
- **Growth**

Obviously, you can't achieve all three with the same investment at the same time. Investments that preserve principal most effectively grow slowly if at all. And any meaningful growth brings with it some risk to principal. What you need is a balance between income and growth.

GO IN THE DIRECTION OF YOUR GOALS

ASSESSING YOUR NEEDS

There are two things you need to know as you evaluate your portfolio: how much you need to live comfortably on your own, and how much income you receive on a regular basis.

In making this assessment, you'll want to think seriously about your own life expectancy and goals. A widow in her 50s, for example, may live 30 years or more, actively involved in work and play a great part of the time. In contrast, a woman in her 80s is likely to have a shorter time to live, if not a less busy lifestyle.

Similarly, if you're still earning a salary, or collecting a pension, you may invest primarily for growth. But if you need additional income to pay living expenses, you may want to concentrate more of your assets in income-producing investments.

The more fully you've considered your situation, the more wisely you can modify your financial plan to make it right for your own needs and goals.

THINGS TO AVOID

While there are no hard and fast rules about what to invest in, there are some things to avoid:

- **Investments that don't let you change your mind at all, or charge you a large fee for doing so**

- **Investments that stress higher yield or higher return than comparable investments. That's a not-too-secret code for risky**

- **Investments whose primary value is reducing taxes**

Something to question are trusts created by your husband's will that are proposed for reasons **other than** reducing estate taxes, especially if they limit your ability to control your own finances after his death. A **marital trust** is often promoted as a way to keep you from worrying about money, which it may do. But it may also prevent you from deciding how to spend it, or to whom you can leave it when you die, even if you survive your husband for many years.

While these types of trusts provide you with income, they are often designed to pass along the bulk of the estate to the next generation. That's one of the reasons trustees tend to be conservative—some would say overly conservative—in their investment choices, since they are compelled by law to act prudently.

SPECIAL (OR NOT SO SPECIAL) INVESTMENTS

If you are worried about cash flow problems as you cope with life as a widow, someone may suggest you consider two approaches tailored for older people. Both have advantages and drawbacks, so you'll want to hear both sides of the story before you decide.

IMMEDIATE ANNUITIES
Immediate annuities pay you income, either for life or a fixed period of time, in exchange for a one-time, lump-sum purchase. An immediate fixed annuity guarantees you a set income, but it will be vulnerable to inflation. An immediate variable annuity gives you the opportunity to get increased income over time, reflecting the growth in your investment portfolios, but the amount of your income will change from time to time and can decline in some periods.

REVERSE MORTGAGES
Reverse mortgages allow you to borrow against the equity in your home, either by receiving regular payments or using a line of credit. It can be an expensive way to borrow money, however, and may be less satisfactory overall than selling the house and renting it from the new owner, or moving to a smaller place.

You can get reverse mortgage information from the American Association of Retired Persons (AARP), the American Bankers Association (ABA) and the Federal Housing Administration (FHA).

MAKING ESTATE PLANS

If you're the primary beneficiary of your husband's estate, it's your responsibility to plan what will happen to your property after you die. Many couples plan together, and draw up wills to reflect those wishes. But things change over time, and you may want to leave your property differently than you once thought.

The first thing to do is draw up a will that makes your current wishes clear. As a widow, you have no obligation to provide for a surviving spouse. However, there can be steep tax consequences depending on the size of your estate. You'll want to work with a lawyer to be sure your intentions are clearly expressed.

Dealing with Illness

You can reduce the financial strain of serious illness by planning ahead.

When you or someone you love is seriously ill, your financial security often suffers as well. And while illness, like divorce and widowhood, is something you'd probably rather not dwell on, there are things you can do ahead of time to reduce its financial impact.

Good health insurance makes a major difference in paying for hospital stays and doctors' visits. Since the most affordable coverage is usually provided by employers, you may want to weigh insurance coverage when you consider job opportunities, especially if one job offers insurance and another doesn't. For example, many advisors caution that even a big increase in salary can be wiped out if you give up comprehensive health insurance to take a job with less coverage, and then get sick or are injured.

In 1996, new rules made it easier for some people to hold on to insurance benefits when they change jobs. But employers are not required to provide health care coverage.

Married couples, however, have the advantage of being covered by each other's plans, so they can select the better one. But you must be careful to check whether your husband's policy will continue to cover you if he should die. Unmarried couples aren't as lucky. Generally, each partner must have individual coverage.

DISABILITY INSURANCE

Health insurance doesn't replace the salary you could lose if you're out of work for an extended period. If you're supporting yourself or others, you may want to consider disability insurance. While you won't receive your full salary, good policies replace about 60% of it, if you meet their qualifying criteria.

The most affordable disability insurance is usually available through your job, or through a professional or social affiliation. It's offered by commercial insurance companies as well. You can ask your financial advisor for help in choosing a policy, but be sure to make comparison shopping part of your search. Prices and coverage can vary widely.

If you pay for your own disability insurance, it's not taxable income. But if your employer pays for it, payments are taxable when you receive them.

MEDICAID: LIMITED HELP

Until your financial resources are almost completely exhausted, you won't qualify for Medicaid assistance in helping to meet your long-term medical bills. While some people try to qualify for this federally sponsored, state-run program by shifting assets to family members or trusts, it's become increasingly difficult to do so. It's risky, therefore, to assume that you don't need to plan for extended illness or the effects of aging.

A CAUTIONARY NOTE—OR TWO

You can help protect yourself and your loved ones from unexpected medical costs by:

- Confirming that your new health insurance coverage is in place before you drop your old plan
- Paying insurance premiums on time so that your coverage isn't dropped
- Arranging for insurance for your children after they finish school or reach age 23 if they don't have coverage through an employer
- Being sure your health insurance is maintained if you're divorced or widowed

ONE AT A TIME

Remember that Medicare coverage is individual, and that you have to be 65 to qualify. If you're married, you and your husband have to apply separately. And if he's eligible before you are, you'll have to be sure you have other insurance until you reach 65. If you're not covered where you work, you can investigate plans available through your husband's employer, through some other group affiliation you might have, or through a commercial insurer or Health Maintenance Organization (HMO). The cost and the coverage can vary dramatically, so you'll probably want to investigate several sources.

LONG-TERM CARE

You can buy long-term care insurance to cover at least part of the cost of extended nursing home care, which is not normally covered by regular health insurance or by Medicare. Some employers offer this insurance at a group rate, and you can also find private coverage—though it tends to be expensive.

Long-term care policies are fairly new, so you'll want to investigate what they cover and how they operate. You'll probably want a policy that has inflation protection, so that inevitable increases in the cost of care are covered. And you'll want to be sure that chronic illnesses like Alzheimer's disease are covered as well.

Experts don't always agree about the most appropriate time to buy long-term care coverage, so you may want to get some different points of view. The time frame that's frequently mentioned is your late 50s to early 60s, after which the cost escalates. In any case, as the coverage becomes more widely available, you should be able to find more competitive prices and more comprehensive plans.

INVESTMENT ALTERNATIVE

Some financial advisors suggest that you use investments rather than insurance to protect yourself if you need large sums for medical and nursing care. Their argument is that you could designate certain long-term growth investments for health-care coverage and build your account regularly, with the premiums you would be paying for insurance. Then, you could convert those investments to income-producers if you needed the money.

The advantage, from their perspective, is that you control what happens to the money. If you need it for health care, you'll have it. And if the need never arises, you can use your nest egg as you please, which you can't do with money you've spent for insurance.

The advocates of the investment approach stress that they're not talking about saving. Money earning minimal interest won't be worth enough to cover the cost of tomorrow's long-term care. The money you're earmarking for this purpose has to increase in value to provide you with what you'll need.

INDEX

INDEX

These notes refer to examples of investment costs, investment performance and to sources of specific information found throughout the text.

* Chart/example is for illustrative purposes only and does not predict past or future performance of any investment.

** Source: © *Stocks, Bonds, Bills and Inflation 1998 Yearbook*, Ibbotson Associates, Chicago (annually updates work by Roger G. Ibbotson and Rex A. Sinquefield). Used with permission. All rights reserved. Stocks are represented by the Standard & Poor's 500 Composite Index, an unmanaged index widely regarded as an indicator of domestic stock market performance. The S&P 500 does not take sales charge into consideration. Investors cannot purchase indices directly. Bonds are represented by long-term government bonds using a one-bond portfolio with a maturity near 20 years. Cash is represented by U.S. Treasury bills rolling over each month a one-bill portfolio containing, at the beginning of each month, the bill having the shortest maturity not less than one month. Inflation is based on the Consumer Price Index. Average annual returns include dividend or interest reinvestment. Past performance does not guarantee future results.

*** Dollar cost averaging plans do not assure a profit or protect against losses in declining markets. Since such plans involve continuous investments regardless of price levels of fund shares, investors should consider their financial ability to continue purchases through periods of low price levels.

TITLES FROM LIGHTBULB PRESS

Available in bookstores everywhere or directly from Lightbulb Press.
Bulk discounts are available. Contact our sales department at 917-256-4900
for more information.

TITLE	PRICE	QUANTITY	SUBTOTAL
The Wall Street Journal Guide to Planning Your Financial Future: The Easy-to-Read Guide to Planning for Retirement ISBN: 0-684-85724-3	$15.95		
The Wall Street Journal Guide to Understanding Money & Investing ISBN: 0-684-86902-0	$15.95		
The Asian Wall Street Journal Guide to Understanding Money & Investing in Asia ISBN: 0-684-84650-0	$14.95		
The Wall Street Journal Guide to Understanding Personal Finance ISBN: 0-684-83361-1	$15.95		
The Wall Street Journal Guide to Understanding Your Taxes ISBN: 0-671-50235-2	$14.95		
A Woman's Guide to Investing ISBN: 0-07-134524-8	$14.95		
Creating Retirement Income ISBN: 0-07-134525-6	$14.95		
Dictionary of Financial Terms ISBN: 0-07-135903-6	$14.95		
User's Guide to the Information Age ISBN: 0-07-134947-2	$14.95		

Sub total _____

Tax (NY only) _____

Shipping* _____

TOTAL DUE _____

* $4 shipping for orders sent to addresses in the Continental US. Actual shipping
charges will apply for 5 or more copies (call for cost). Sorry, no international orders.

SHIPPING INFORMATION

Name _____

Address _____ Apt. _____

City _____ State __ Zip _____

Daytime phone _____

BILLING INFORMATION
(for credit card orders only)

Name _____

Address _____ Apt. _____

City _____ State __ Zip _____

Daytime phone _____

__ AmEx __ MasterCard __ Visa

Account number _____

Expiration date _____

WITH A CREDIT CARD
Call 800-581-9884.

ON THE INTERNET
Visit our website at **www.lightbulbpress.com**.

BY MAIL
Complete this form and send it with a **money order** payable to **Lightbulb Press** for the total due to the address shown below. Checks or cash cannot be accepted.

BY FAX
Complete this form, include your credit card information, and fax it to the number shown below.

LIGHTBULB PRESS, INC.
112 Madison Avenue
New York, NY 10016
www.lightbulbpress.com
Phone 917-256-4900
Fax   917-256-4949